A GUIDE TO
CONFIDENT LIVING

By Norman Vincent Peale

FAWCETT CREST • NEW YORK

INTRODUCTION

Over a considerable period, the author has had the opportunity to work with large numbers of people facing modern problems in the heart of America's greatest city. He has conducted a consultation service in the Marble Collegiate Church on Fifth Avenue, New York, to which hundreds of people every year come for help and guidance. The staff consists of ministers, psychiatrists, physicians and social psychiatrists.

The author has evolved a specific technique designed to lead people to personal happiness and success. This method has worked for the many who have put it into practice. Its efficiency has been amply demonstrated; it has been tested and found satisfactory by hundreds of people. It has produced amazing results in the personal experience of many. It has indeed proved a guide to confident living.

Yet the principles of happiness and success to be presented in this book are not new. They were not created by the author but are as old as the Bible. In fact they are the simple principles taught in the Bible. If the techniques possess any uniqueness, it lies in the effort to show HOW to use these principles in a practical and understanding manner suited to modern men.

The book may seem repetitious at times. That is because it is a text book of a formula. It hammers on one basic procedure and repetition is the master of studies, as the classic saying goes. Reiteration is essential in persuading the reader to practice; to try and try again. If water wears away a stone, so does emphasis, even at the danger of repetition, wear away our apathy toward self-betterment.

This book is not theoretical. It contains the detailed description of a technique of living that can lead those who definitely put it into operation to success and happiness. The book is written with one primary purpose: to state and demonstrate a simple, workable technique of thinking and acting that has revitalized the lives of thousands of moderns. The important substance in the book is the how-ness. It tells HOW you can achieve your most cherished desires.

This book presents in simple outline those formulas which make life work successfully. Each chapter deals with an aspect of the unified theme of the book, namely, HOW...to be happy and successful. The tested method is applied to some of the basic causes of unhappiness and failure: tension, fear, inferiority, wrong thinking, and other mental handicaps.

Not every factor in successful and happy living is discussed, for that is neither possible nor necessary. The formula is applied to enough factors, however, to teach the reader *how* to use techniques which are applicable to all situations. The method is sufficiently developed to show the reader what he wants to know—how to be happy and successful. This book is offered as a guide to confident living.

NORMAN VINCENT PEALE

CONTENTS

TO MY CHILDREN:

Margaret

John

and

Elizabeth

Chapter One

A NEW-OLD WAY TO
FREE YOUR POWERS

A young and highly trained physician sometimes writes an apparently curious prescription for people afflicted with the maladies described in this book: fear, inferiority, tension and kindred troubles. His prescription is—"Go to church at least once a Sunday for the next three months."

To the surprised and mystified patient to whom he has given this astonishing prescription, he explains that in a church there are a mood and atmosphere containing healing power that will help cure him of the troubles I have just mentioned. He further asserts that he does not particularly care whether the patient listens to the sermon. Church going is of value if a person merely sits quietly, yielding himself to the mood and atmosphere of the church. This modern physician reports that amazing benefits have come to his patients as a result of this practice.

A woman, a long-time friend of the doctor's family, was the type of patient who goes from doctor to doctor, never giving heed, never putting into practice the advice received. Finally she came to this doctor and he told her frankly, "I don't want your case." When she asked him why, he replied, "Simply because you will not do what I tell you."

She begged and insisted and promised faithfully she would

do as he prescribed, but still he demurred. In a final plea she said, "I have the money to pay for your services and how can you as a doctor refuse my case?"

So he consented on one condition: she must do exactly as he prescribed without argument and with full cooperation. He even made her sign a paper to that effect.

The reason she was in such a nervous condition was because her sister had married the man whom she wanted to marry and she hated her sister. Her entire personality was simmering and the hate poisons were unsettling her to such an extent that her whole system reacted and she had actual symptoms of sickness. The doctor gave her some medicine because he knew that was what she wanted—the first day pink, the second day white pills.

Finally one day the doctor wrote the prescription described above. When she looked at it, amazement overspread her countenance and she snapped, "That is the silliest thing I ever heard of. I won't do it. What are you anyway, a doctor or a preacher?"

The doctor took out the paper she had signed and said, "You must do it or I am through with your case."

Grudgingly she followed directions. Some time elapsed before any benefit was apparent because of the antagonisms in her mind, but presently even she began to yield herself to the healing atmosphere and curative mood present in a service of worship.

One day to her surprise and despite her antipathy, she found herself interested in the sermon. She answered it keenly, discovering to her astonishment that it was common sense. It appealed to her tremendously. Her interest grew, she became docile to the ministrations of the physician and presently, due to this wise combination of medical practice and religion, resentment went out of her and health came in.

"So you see, my prescription works," said the doctor. In this case he also prescribed religious reading. Gradually the idea of Christianity as a technique and a scientific mechanism designed to overcome the problems to be treated in this book began to dominate her mind. Today this woman has a firm grip on life and is a well person, not only physically but emotionally and spiritually, for it was in the latter areas of her life that the poison was being generated.

Another doctor has on several occasions sent patients to my church. These people are not physically ill but are so filled with fears, anxieties and tensions, feelings of guilt, inferiority and resentment that, like the woman described above, they are properly called sick.

He sent one man who had not been to church in years and when the doctor told the man to go to church, the patient resisted, saying, "I detest sermons."

"Go to church anyway," the doctor said, "and don't listen to the sermon. Take cotton along if you wish and put it in your ears when the sermon begins. But there is one thing I want you to do. In that church every Sunday morning and evening they have a period of quietness, which they call 'the period of creative silence.' The minister will suggest that you yield yourself to this quietness and open your mind to the recreative power of God which has the power to permeate the soul, bringing benign and healing influence. The minister will be entirely correct in saying that and it will be a medicine far better than anything I can give you. It is the only way I know out of your difficulties. Therefore that is the medicine which I prescribe for your condition."

This man followed directions and the doctor reports that now he, too, is listening to the sermon. In fact, he finds himself intensely interested in the church. He never dreamed it would make such an appeal to him. A definite change for the better is beginning to come over him.

"By giving these patients the advice to go to church, I am utilizing a technique that works in many maladies. I have learned that in treating a human being we must consider the whole man and deal with him as something other than a mechanism or organism, for man is more than a bundle of chemical reactions. I believe," said the doctor, "that faith plus science properly correlated can do tremendous good."

An explanation of the phenomena described by this physician lies in the effectiveness of group therapy. Psychiatrists and psychologists not only utilize consultation and psychological treatment in working privately with individuals, but under certain circumstances they also make use of group treatment for several patients at one time. In such circumstances the counselor is working with people who have a common background in personal counseling. They are therefore familiar with the usual procedures and know how to cooperate fully.

In the instance of a service of public worship, the minister who during the week is a private counselor, attempts to bring to bear upon the members of a large congregation similar techniques for applying spiritual power except that now he uses group therapy. His congregation is composed of many types. Some are present because they realize their need of help. Others need help but are not conscious of it. Still others are present merely out of habit. Others may be present because they unconsciously seek some satisfying answer to the vague dissatisfactions of their minds.

In a large congregation, while there is a wide diversification of interest, it is also true that there are only a few basic human problems. It must also be taken into consideration that people are people regardless of who they are or what their backgrounds may be. There are certain deep universal appeals to human interest and to these human nature always responds. There is no force equal to religion in its power to touch and to satisfy basic needs. For this reason the personal religious counselor and the religious practitioner of group therapy have an opportunity enjoyed by no other scientist in the field to reach to the depths of human nature and thus bring healing strength, peace and power.

May I outline my own practice? The above mentioned theories began to develop in my mind some years ago as the number of persons with whom I was privately counseling increased. I came to the ministry of a Fifth Avenue church at the low point of the depression, back in 1932. New York City, as the financial center of the nation, was profoundly affected by the depression and I soon became aware of the fear, anxiety, insecurity, disappointment, frustration, and failure everywhere at hand. I began to preach on these themes and stressed how faith in God could give courage and wisdom together with new insights for the solution of problems. Advertising such topics in the press brought large congregations to hear these discussions. Soon my schedule of personal interviews was more than I could possibly handle and long waiting lists developed. Recognizing my lack of specialized knowledge, I turned to a highly competent psychiatrist, Dr. Smiley Blanton, for help and thus began the counseling clinic in the church.

Soon I began to notice in the congregation scores of people with whom I had counseled personally. It was then that the thought came of carrying over from the interview room to a big congregation the same technique of spiritual treatment we were utilizing in personal consultation.

One technique used in the service of public worship which has produced amazing results is the period of directed quietness. Attendance at Quaker meetings had taught me the value of creative silence. In meeting with the Friends, I derived great personal benefit such as lowering of tension, strength over fear and mental clarification which helped me in one or two instances to most astounding solution of problems. The Friends, of course, have the advantage of long years of training in the tradition of silent meditation. We in the churches generally have never developed expertness in utilizing quietness in worship. Protestants as a rule do not practice complete quietness but inevitably have a background of music. I began to interject complete silence but did it gradually and only occasionally; it proved so effective that now if I omit it for one service many people are sure to protest.

The technique which we employ was described in a pamphlet issued by the Marble Collegiate Church Sermon Publication Committee:

Picture the church filled to overflowing by a great congregation numbering more than 2000 people. The sunlight is streaming in the great windows, illuminating the sanctuary and falling softly upon the worshipping multitude. The church interior is a combination of gold and soft reds, with red brocade cushions and back rests in the mahogany and white colonial pews. Around three sides the great balcony swings.

The front of the church is not in the form of an altar, but a small platform on which are placed three large, stately chairs, against a backdrop of rich red velvet. At the left of the platform is a beautiful lectern on which rests the great pulpit Bible. Towering above and behind the backdrop is a great nave which carries out the gold decoration. Here sits the choir. Dr. Peale is seated in the large center chair, his associates on either side.

Following the reading of the Scripture, a deep hush settles upon the congregation. Dr. Peale arises, steps to the front of the platform and with nothing between himself and the congregation he speaks somewhat as follows: "We have come here this morning because God is in this place and we want to make contact with Him. This greatest of all experiences possible to human beings is best accomplished through silence. It is possible for every person in this Church to now establish a close contact with God that he shall be recreated. Remember the words of the Scriptures, 'In Him we live, and move, and have our being.' As long as we are 'in Him' we are in the flow of God's power and strength. Peace and power are ours. But sadly we become detached from this flow. We do not live 'in Him' and thus accumulate fear, anxiety, negative thinking—everything that causes failure. Let us, therefore, practice now a moment of absolute silence. I suggest that you allow your body to assume a relaxed position in order that tension may go out of you. Perhaps you may wish to close your eyes to shut out the world. In this moment of silence, the one thing you must not do is to think about yourself or any of your problems. Instead, think about God for one minute and conceive of Him as now recreating you. Let us retire into a vital and vibrant period of creative meditation."

So saying, a deep silence falls upon the congregation. If there has been any coughing up to this point, it ceases. The only sound you can hear is the swish of automobile tires on the Avenue outside and even that seems far away.

It is not a dead silence, for there is aliveness and vibrancy in the air. There is always the spirit of expectancy that something great is about to happen. Sometimes this silence lasts only for sixty seconds. Sometimes longer, but people become lost in the silence. It is as if God, Himself, touches their minds with peace.

Presently in a very quiet voice, Dr. Peale breaks the silence by saying: "Come unto me, all ye that labor and are heavy laden, and I will give you rest." And he also adds, "Thou wilt keep him in perfect peace, whose mind is stayed on thee." He stresses this latter verse, emphasizing that for the period of quietness the minds of the worshippers have been fixed not upon their troubles but upon God. And because of that firm fixing of their minds upon the Eternal, God has sent His peace to them in that period of silence.

Scores of people report that the most amazing benefits have occurred to them in this quiet period. Strangely enough, it is not as you might expect, women who seen to appreciate this period of quietness, but the hard-pressed business man of today expresses himself enthusiastically as to the benefits he receives. Perhaps this in part at least accounts for the fact that the congregations in the Marble Collegiate Church are more than fifty per cent men.

I am convinced that in the vibrant and healing silence which falls over a great congregation when the suggestion is emphasized and accepted that God is present and that Jesus Christ walks the aisles to touch human beings, actual power is being released.

We know that the universe is filled with power, that the very air is charged with it. Only a short time ago we discovered atomic energy. Other forms of energy which shall subsequently be developed may even be greater. Cannot we then assume that in this dynamic universe there are spiritual forces all about us ready to play upon us and to recreate us? The New Testament definitely assures us that spiritual power is a fact. Christianity is more than a promise of power. It is power itself. The New Testament declares, "As many as received him, to them gave he power." Again it states, "Ye shall receive power, after the Holy Spirit is come upon you." All of which means that when an individual conditions his mind to the illimitable spirit of power which fills the universe, it shall fill him also.

The New Testament tells us that Christianity is life, not a way of life, but life itself. It is the essence of life. It is vitality and vibrant energy. Christianity is, therefore, more than a creed or an idea. It is a throbbing, pulsating, vibrant, creative energy even in such manner as the sunlight is energy, only infinitely more so. It is a deep therapy which can drive to the heart of a personality or of society (which is an amalgamation of individual personalities) in breaking down infection centers, building up life centers, transforming, endowing with new energy—in a word, recreating. "In him was life; and the life was the light of men." "In him," that is in Christ, is life (vitality). "In him" is creative energy and this creative energy is the tremendous dynamic power of life itself.

We do not half realize the tremendous power with which we may make contact when in church. But when we drive deeply into Christianity, as in a service of worship such as described, and gradually yield to the atmosphere, we become relaxed in body, mind and spirit. The hymns, the choral music, the reading from the Bible, the quiet, unhurried mood all conspire to conditioning the mind for the period of silence. When by a conscious act of will one turns his mind to God, fixing his thought upon the divine source of power and energy; then in such manner as if he had turned a switch and electrical contact had been made, spiritual power begins to pass into him.

I call attention to a network of wires which draw electrical energy out of the universe. This power illuminates the church. It operates the pipe organ. It controls the heating unit. By means of thermostatic control of this power, the heat flow comes and goes as needed. Electrical energy operates the loud speaker system to carry the service to overflow auditoriums in the same building. The entire structure is a network of wires which constitute in themselves the medium over which power flows. Isn't it a reasonable assumption that such a building where many minds are unified in concentration on the same objective is also a great reception center for power far greater than electricity? Two thousand mental and spiritual antennae draw spiritual power to this congregation and this power enters the minds, bodies and souls of those who have become attuned to this mystic yet real force.

Another central factor of Christianity employed in spiritual therapy is the thought of light. It is interesting to observe the frequent references to light in the New Testament. It is usually related to new life. Men have discovered the extraordinary healing properties of light in healing. Touch a wire containing two hundred volts and get a shock. Touch a wire over which is passing twenty-five thousand volts and you will be electrocuted, but make contact with one million volts and instead of destroying you, the contact will build up your body cells. Under the infra-red lamp in two minutes you can derive perhaps as much therapeutic benefit as by exposing yourself for one hour to direct sunlight, since the dust in the atmosphere weakens the value of the sunlight. Thus light is used in healing.

Judged by its healing effect, Christianity possesses the same quality. The Bible tell us that in Jesus Christ is life and this life is the "light" of men which can heal and transform them so that they themselves are filled with new and recreated life.

In applying group therapy in services of public worship, many individuals are exposed to creative light energy in a spiritual sense. I want always to be on the side of common sense and factual realities. A crank is abhorrent to me. I believe always in being truly and completely scientific and rational in religious faith and practice. This does not mean, however, that one must be bound by materialistic science. Christianity, as will repeatedly be pointed out in this book, is itself a science. I positively believe, therefore, that if a man will go to church and attune himself to the mood and atmosphere and if for one minute of silence he will turn from the negative and destructive thoughts that agitate his mind and, if truly relaxed in body and in soul, he will affirm faith in

God, he thereby opens himself to the recreative power that flows constantly through the universe.

After such a service, I received a letter from a very rational and intelligent woman:

I want to tell you how much your services mean to me. It is an inspiration to attend a service in the Marble Church and I feel that it is to those services that I owe the fact that I am well now.

For five years I have had attacks of insomnia and a nervous breakdown. Last fall I returned to my position after being ill all summer. In desperation I thought I would try to work again.

After six weeks of every day being a misery, and after three times offering to resign, I went to a service in the Marble Church. You had the silent prayer before which you told the congregation how to pray and how to cast out all worry and how to let the mind receive the power of God to take over worries. The sermon was along the same line.

I went out of church feeling much better. I prayed often for help and guidance and on Wednesday of the following week, I suddenly realized that I felt all right and I have been so ever since. I began to enjoy my work. After a few weeks I began to sleep without taking any medicine. At your church service I found the clue for curing myself by your showing me how to let God help me.

This woman came to church a defeated, baffled, disorganized person. Apparently she was of that mental and spiritual quality which enabled her to become sufficiently childlike and naive to follow with faith the suggested procedures. The tremendous power of faith came to the forefront of her mind and faith is the contact point with God's power. As she sat in church relaxed, yielding and believing, the healing light of God began to encompass her. It proceeded into her life by its deep therapy. It took away the sense of strain. Her nerves relaxed. It penetrated into her mind, deep into her tortured and tormented being. It reached the spot from which her trouble was coming. It spread throughout her mind a healing radiance and she was changed.

A friend gave me an excellent definition of a competent church service: "The creation of an atmosphere in which a spiritual miracle can take place." Tremendous things happen to personality under such circumstances when the mood is auspicious.

I heard a charming young woman say that she was sitting rather indolently in the congregation when the preacher shot out these words, "God has the power to take an ordinary person and make him extraordinary if that person will yield himself completely to the power of God."

This struck her with great force, so much so that it revolutionized her thinking. A change began to take place in a personality hitherto ineffective and she became one of the most amazing persons I have ever known. She developed unusual charm, superior leadership abilities and such an infectious spiritual life that scores of people have been changed by contact with her. With all of this, she is a person of rare personal qualities, having all of the gifts and graces of a modern woman. In any group, she is "the life of the party."

A man wrote me following a service of worship. His trouble was mental confusion. He was in New York for a conference which involved the future of a business. A heavy investment was involved in the negotiations. All day Thursday,

Friday and Saturday he and his associates struggled for an answer but without results. This man was wise enough to understand that a sustained tension of mind instead of producing clarification tends toward continued bafflement. You have to break the tension of thought sometimes and relax your mind to get an idea through. So that Sunday he came to church and heard the minister suggest that all problems be dropped from the mind for one minute and that everyone turn his thoughts to God. This businessman had never previously heard this procedure advocated but the logic of it appealed to him and he followed precisely the directions given. He was an expert in his business and he had come to church on the assumption that the church provides expert spiritual treatment, so he followed directions expecting results and he got results.

He states that all of a sudden like a spotlight moving across a dark theater to light upon some particular object on the stage, itself blacked out, the answer to his problem stood out in his mind distinct and completely formulated. Unquestionably the sustained thought which he had given to his problem throughout the previous days had been formulating an answer in his mind but the releasing of the answer was accomplished by relaxing his mind through spiritual therapy.

Take another man, one prominent in the financial life of New York. He asked me to visit his firm in the Wall Street district where I found a very prosperous and important business being carried on under his direction. After showing me his interesting offices and describing his outstanding work, he made this surprising statement, "Most of the people who work for me are making more money for themselves and this business has attained new heights all because of something that happened to me in your church."

He had come to church one Sunday morning and had fully entered into the spirit of the service. His mind, which is very active and alert, became attuned. Of a sudden into his mind flashed an idea. It was a complete outline of profit sharing that would allow certain people to go far beyond their existing salaries. He immediately put this plan into operation with the result that not only does each person participating in the plan make more money, but the firm has gone away ahead of any previous records. The best place on earth to get a new and workable idea for your business is in the type of church service described in this chapter.

Such amazing power can thus be generated that we hear often of people's lives being completely changed, sometimes instantly, in church services. Undoubtedly the reader has read stories of dramatic conversions which have been validated in the subsequent life of the individual for long years even to the day they die. The explanation of these phenomena is that these persons made contact with a power developed through mood and atmosphere and faith that at the proper conjuncture affected the individual so tremendously that previous habits were broken, the individual becoming as the New Testament graphically says, "A new creature: old things are passed away; behold, all things become new."

The congregation of my own church over a period of several years has been trained in this technique. However, this congregation is composed at every service of hundreds of visitors, many of whom find this procedure entirely new. They, too, report that when they yield themselves in full cooperation to the spiritual force to which appeal is being made, amazing results are obtained.

Not long ago I attempted to apply this therapy to a large congregation in a Southern city before which I had never spoken. The members of this congregation were totally unacquainted with this form of Christian procedure. I was preaching on the text, "Hear, and your soul shall live." I stated that "to hear" means more than merely to listen with the outer ear. The word has a deep content, implying the complete enthrallment of the mind to the presence of God. I pointed out that it means to hear not alone with the ear but also with the very essence of the mind. I explained that "to hear" means to believe that something is being said that has the power to drive to the center of your nature and release you from any crippling thing which may dwarf or frustrate your personality.

I asked the members of this large congregation to conceive of God's power as flowing through the church and playing down upon them. I urged each person during one minute of silence to turn from every problem in his mind and to listen intently not to me, the speaker, but to Jesus Christ and to practice "hearing" His words, "Come unto me, all ye that labor and are heavy laden, and I will give you rest."

I ceased speaking and stood still while a deathlike hush fell upon the vast assemblage. Afterwards a man came to me and stated that he had attended church for years but that even so his mind continued to be filled with fears and worries and that since boyhood he had suffered from a lack of confidence in himself. "All my life," he said, "I have been inwardly and emotionally bound up and though I have become fairly successful, it has been despite myself rather than because of it. I have suffered inner conflict all my life but," he asserted as he looked at me with an expression of incredulity on his face, "during that moment when you asked the people to really listen, I became completely lost and enthralled. When it was over I came to, but in the moment that I was lost, I found myself. I feel as if some power has rushed through me carrying out with it that which has troubled me for years. I believe that at last I am free."

What had happened to him was simply that he had made contact with a force so great that it permeated the controlling areas of the mind and made him over. This power, namely, God, created him in the first place and that power is always present to keep recreating us if the contact is not broken but is firmly maintained. When it *is* broken, fears and defeats surge in to dominate the personality; if the contact is reestablished, these destructive elements are flushed out and the person again begins to live. In this case the operation seemed to be instantaneous, as it often is. Sometimes it requires cultivation over a period, but always it marks the recreation of the individual.

We shall proceed to outline a simple but workable technique for successful living. As stated in the Introduction, nothing is offered here on a theoretical basis. Every principle in this book has been worked out in verifiable laboratory tests. These principles will work when they are worked. Confidence in these teachings is based on the fact that they had been developed out of the lives of real people, not once but many times. They have the effect of law because they have been proven by repeated demonstration. Let me drive home this fact: *If you will utilize the principles of faith stated in this book, you, too, can solve the difficult problems of your personality. You, too, can really learn to live.* It is not important what church you attend—Protestant, Catholic, or Jewish—nor does it make any difference how much you have failed in the past or how unhappy your present state of mind. Regardless of how apparently hopeless your condition may be, if you will believe in the principles outlined in this book and seriously start to work with them, you will get positive results.

I urge you to consider carefully the amazing things that often happen in church and suggest that you submit yourself not only to the private therapy of faith but to the astounding effect that group therapy may have upon you.

But to attend church successfully, skill is required. Worship is not a hit or miss affair. There is an art to it. Those who by study and practice become expert in church going master one of the greatest of all skills, that of spiritual power. That you may learn to go to church efficiently. I suggest the following ten rules to guide you in mastering the art of church going. Consistently put these rules into practice and one of these days the great thing may happen to you.

1. Think of church going as an art, with definite rules to follow, an art you can acquire.
2. Go regularly to church. A prescription designed by a physician to be taken at regular intervals is not effective if taken once a year.
3. Spend a quiet Saturday evening and get a good sleep. Get in condition for Sunday.
4. Go in a relaxed state of body and mind. Don't rush to church. Go in a leisurely manner. The absence of tension is a requisite of successful worship.
5. Go in a spirit of enjoyment. Church is not a place of gloom. Christianity is a radiant and happy thing. Re-

ligion should be enjoyed.

6. Sit relaxed in the pew, feet on floor, hands loosely in lap or at the side. Allow the body to yield to the contour of the pew. Don't sit rigid. God's power cannot get through to your personality through a tied-up body and mind.

7. Don't bring a "problem" to church. Think hard during the week, but let the problem "simmer" in the mind over Sunday. God's peace brings creative energy to help in the intellectual process. You will receive insight to solve your problem.

8. Do not bring ill will to church. A grudge blocks the flow of spiritual power. To cast out ill will, pray in church for those you do not like or who dislike you.

9. Practice the art of spiritual contemplation. In church do not think about yourself. Think about God. Think of some beautiful and peaceful thing, perhaps even of the stream where you fished last summer. The idea is to get mentally away from the world, into an atmosphere of peace and refreshment.

10. Go to church expecting some great thing to happen to you. Believe that a church service is the creation of an atmosphere in which a spiritual miracle can take place. Men's lives have been changed in church through faith in Christ. Believe it can happen to you.

I could summon scores of people to testify to the great things that happen in church to change people's lives. However, one stands out unforgettably in my mind. Early one Monday morning I received a telephone call from a gentleman who asked if I had received the card mailed to the church the night before. We have in our pews simply worded cards upon which an individual may register his desire to begin practicing the spiritual life.

This man stated that he had signed a card the night before and urged me to come to see him at once. He was so insistent that it apparently meant so much to him that I left my office and went to see him. I found that he was the controller of a large business organization. He was surrounded by all of the accoutrements of an important man and occupied a spacious office. He was a quiet, dignified man, one of the most impressive personalities I have ever known.

"Something has happened which has changed everything and I simply had to talk to you about it at once because it happened in your church last night."

He then launched into the story of his experience, talking in a quiet manner, though intense excitement was evident beneath the surface of his calmness. "I am not a church man," he asserted. "In fact, rarely have I gone to church over the past twenty years. I have been too busy, or at least I thought I was. For some few years now I have had the feeling that something is lacking, yet I seemed to have everything—money, position, friends, influence and power; but you know how it is, how sometimes your food just doesn't taste right. Well, life did not taste right to me. The flavor was not as fine as when I was younger. I have lived a fairly decent life and there is nothing dramatic in what happened to me in the way of turning from sin, for I really have no sins of a very serious nature. It was just that my life doesn't thrill me any more— that is, until last night." Then he began to recite the same old story of tension, fear, irritability, antagonism, as characteristic of his daily trouble. These things he apparently did not consider as sins but they were the root cause of the dissatisfaction with which he had been afflicted.

"At any rate," he continued, "I happened to be walking down Fifth Avenue last night and passed your church. The topic on the bulletin board attracted me and I decided to go in. I came in late and the only seat I could find was in the rear of the balcony. The first thing that surprised me was that the church was filled. I did not think that people went to church any more, especially on Sunday night but then, you see, it has been a long time and I know very little about churches.

"I found myself yielding to the mood and atmosphere of the place. It was homey and friendly. A feeling of satisfaction began to come over me and I really had a peaceful feeling too. In your sermon you were driving home the point that if anybody in that great congregation had anything bothering them, that they could have the matter settled if they would turn their minds to God. I imagine that is a crude way of expressing what you said, but that is the idea I got. You were very positive in your assertion and illustrated your sermon by the stories of people who had done that and to whom something great had happened. I was intensely interested in those stories and suddenly I became aware that what had happened to those people was what I wanted to have happen to me. You then stated that there was a card in the pew upon which one could register his desire to have this happen.

"I took that card in my hand but could not bring myself to sign it. But I put it in my pocket and went back to my hotel, went to bed and to sleep. In the middle of the night I was suddenly wide awake. It was shortly after three A.M. I struggled to go to sleep but a strange excitement seemed to possess me, and I arose and sat in my chair. The memory of the church service came back and suddenly I thought of the card. I laid it on my desk and re-read it. As I did so I knew that I must sign that card. I found myself praying. I signed the card.

"Then I felt that I must mail it at once to you, so I put on my bathrobe and walked down the hall to the mail chute and stood there holding the card. For a moment I hesitated. It was so strange that I, Bill ————, should be doing such a thing. Had I suddenly become emotional! Had I grown old? Was I turning to religion in my old age, but fifty-six isn't old, is it?

"Then I opened my fingers and dropped the card. For just a second I could see it flash down the mail chute and then it was gone."

He turned a very intense gaze upon me. "The minute I dropped that card, something happened to me. I became inexpressibly happy." Saying this he dropped his head on the desk and to my surprise began to sob. I am always embarrassed to hear a man cry and I simply sat still and let him sob. Finally he raised his head and without even apologizing said, "It seems that my whole life all of a sudden is broken up and I am so happy that I wanted you to come over here at once so that I could tell you about it. From this time on I know the answer to all my problems. I have found peace and happiness."

This gentleman lived for three years after this time, but always I shall remember him as one of the greatest personalities I ever knew. He went to church and something great happened to him which changed everything for him.

And this same thing happens in churches everywhere every Sunday, or for that matter whenever a church service is held. Put yourself in the way of it—it can happen to you.

And now—an important reminder—fix this though firmly in your mind until it dominates your consciousness: *You do not need to be defeated by anything.* Your life can be a great experience. The methods and techniques suggested in this book will work *if you work them.*

Chapter Two

DON'T KEEP YOUR TROUBLES
TO YOURSELF

At a railroad station newsstand my attention was drawn to an extensive display of magazines and books dealing with the common problems of living.

"I notice you have a great deal of this literature for sale," I commented to the salesgirl.

"Yeah," she slangily replied, "and I'm tellin' you that kind of stuff sure does sell."

"More than murder mysteries or movie magazines?" I inquired.

"Yeah, more than all of those, and they even outtop the love stories. Believe me," she declared, "this self-improvement or self-help literature is what we count on to pay the profits of this business."

"What is the reason?" I asked.

"The answer's easy," she replied. "The poor things (referring to her customers) are all tangled up. There are so many things they want to get away from, mostly themselves, I suppose." Then she paused. "I guess they're looking for someone to release them from all their troubles."

One learns not to be be surprised at wisdom from unexpected sources. An observant salesgirl daily serving the public may develop shrewd insights into the ways of human nature and the needs of human beings.

As I walked away, her wise words rang in my ears: "The poor things are all tangled up. They are looking for someone to release them from all their troubles."

Of course, it is a very large order but somebody has to perform this function of release for modern people. To meet the situation, a whole new profession has developed, that of personal counseling. It is not in the strict sense new for there have always been men who have dealt with personal problems. However, it is only within recent years that it has become a specialized undertaking. Human beings of late seem to have developed higher tension, greater nervousness, deeper fears, profounder anxieties and more severe neuroses and complexes. It is one of the marked characteristics of our time. Some antidote being positively required, the personal counseling service has been developed. It is performed largely by psychiatrists, psychologists, clergymen, social workers, and of course physicians.

It must be borne in mind that the beneficiaries of this new profession are not people of distorted mental life or pathological persons. The profession's primary function is to keep normal people normal. Counseling is basically preventative rather than curative, but it is also curative. It deals with the common fears, anxieties, hates and guilt reactions of everyday people. Modern man is beginning to realize that primarily it is in his thoughts that his happiness and efficiency are determined; he is learning that the condition of his emotional health indicates whether or not he shall have peace, serenity and strength. And mental, emotional and spiritual health are essential to success in living.

Experts in personal efficiency know that to be successful

in business, or in any kind of work, it is necessary to be a well integrated, well-organized personality. Men fail not alone because of laziness or lack of ability, but there are deeper causes of failure in the mental attitudes and emotional reactions. In most instances the average person does not understand these reactions and their fundamental influence upon all his actions. The trained counselor helps a person to know himself, to understand why he does what he does. He teaches a person to analyze his motives, his objectives and his reactions. If it is a good practice to go to your dentist, or to your physician periodically, it is equally wise to go to your spiritual advisor for regular checkups. When you begin to feel troubled and your personality seems to be disorganized, go to your counselor and frankly tell him what is troubling you. He may be able to release you from these unhappy factors which make you one of that vast number whom the salesgirl characterized as "poor things, they are all tangled up."

Through an example, I can make plain the scientific attitude that underlies religious counseling. A man, who was a victim of nerves, came for an interview. His mind was in such a panic that he could no longer do his work. He occupied an important position but had completely lost his grip. He was not suffering a nervous breakdown but was moving rapidly toward that condition. His doctor told him frankly that he had no medicine for him except sedatives. He recommended that he see a psychiatrist, but as the patient was leaving the office, the doctor reconsidered. "Maybe you had better see a minister," he advised. The thought had just flashed across the physician's mind that perhaps this man's trouble was in the sphere where the minister practices.

"In a certain sense," said the physician, "ministers are also doctors. That is to say, they are physicians of the soul and it is often the troubles of the soul that make us sick in mind and spirit and sometimes in the body as well."

The patient came to see me. He was not a member of my church, nor had I ever met him. Indeed I knew nothing about him whatsoever. After a brief discussion, it became obvious that he needed to make a confession which I encouraged him to do. After he had cleansed his thoughts completely, and he had plenty in his mind to make him sick, I asked, "Why didn't you see your own minister about this?"

"Oh," he said, with a shocked expression, "I know him too well."

"What do you mean, you know him too well?" I asked.

"Why," he said, "you see, he is a close friend of mine. Our families have dinner together ever so often. His children know my children, and why," he added rather lamely, "he is my pastor. He would be shocked to hear these things."

"You always try to put your best foot forward with your pastor, is that it?"

"Why, certainly," he replied, "that is what everyone does with his minister. You just don't want your minister to know anything bad about you."

"You are not very friendly with your doctor, I take it."

"Why, of course, the doctor is as good a friend of mine as the minister."

"Has your doctor ever operated on you?" I asked.

"Oh, yes, twice."

"Then your doctor knows you inside and out. There is nothing about you that is hidden from him, is there? But you are not embarrassed before him, are you, when you go out to dinner. You do not think as you watch the doctor across the table that he is sitting there saying gleefully, 'Ah, I have seen that fellow's insides. I know just what they look like.' Of course, the doctor has no time to keep your insides on his mind. It is a professional matter with him. He sees you as a patient and in such interviews he is largely the scientist, though, of course, he has a personal interest in you. When he is with you socially, he thinks of you only as a friend, not as a patient. He has a right, in the periods of social and friendly intercourse, to be relieved of his professional duties which require him to think of people's ills and their insides.

"So," I continued, "surely you do not think that when the minister goes out to dinner with you, that he is sitting across the table saying, 'Ah, I remember what he told me about himself. I know something he did. I know all about his moral and spiritual insides.' What is true of the doctor is also true of the minister. He, too, wants to enjoy friendly relationships when he is socially engaged. He sees so much of the pain, trouble, and evil of life that when he finishes with his interviews he wants relief from all of it; therefore, he has trained himself to cast them out of his mind.

"Remember that the minister is also a professional man. When he is dealing with a human being in the relation of pastor and parishioner, he is applying all of his spiritual, psychological and scientific knowledge. He is entirely objective, viewing the person whom he is interviewing as a patient to whom he must apply a cure. When later he meets that same person socially, the chances are that what he was told in the interview never enters his mind. I know from experience that people have come to me six months or a year after I first interviewed them and I could not for the life of me remember a single detail of their story.

"That is only natural," I pointed out, "because I see a great many people and could not possibly burden my mind with all the details of everything that everybody tells me. I would have a nervous breakdown if I tried that. The minister who counsels with people, cannot in the very nature of the case keep such matters in his mind."

Personally I do not even keep a "case history." No written records are made. The interview is completely confidential. If a person returns for counseling and previously related facts are not recalled, it is necessary for the individual to retell the story to freshen my mind regarding the problem.

There is also in the relation of the minister with his parishioners the background idea of the father and his children. The Catholic church emphasizes that the priest is the spiritual father and the church the great mother of mankind. The priest as father represents the mother church which exercises care over her spiritual children. Protestants have never held this concept but that which is told to a minister is kept, of course, in complete and sacred confidence. There will never be even the slightest breaking of any confidence reposed in him as a pastor. The minister also acts for God in his sacred capacity as spiritual shepherd of the congregation.

It is important to think of the minister as a scientific person to whom one can talk as freely and as confidentially as with a doctor. His true position in the community can be called that of a scientist of the spiritual life, especially trained for his particular function. He has as much right to "hang out his shingle" as any other scientifically trained man, not for the practice of medicine, for never would he infringe upon the function of the medical healer, but for practice in his own sphere; he should be looked upon in the community as a skilled, well-trained scientific man—a shepherd of human souls, a physician of personality.

A prominent physician, Dr. James H. Means of the Massachusetts General Hospital, and Professor of Clinical Medicine at Harvard University, said, "The patient, when he is sick, should send for his minister as quickly as he sends for his doctor." Therefore, do not think of the minister merely socially. Do not overly emphasize the sacred or pious character of his calling. Do not be embarrassed to frankly tell him everything. He has heard of and probably has dealt with every problem and every sin that you may mention. There is nothing you have ever done or can do that has not at some previous time come before him as a human problem. He does not become shocked nor does he lose his regard and respect for you for he has a deep and philosophical understanding of human nature. Despite whatever evil you may confess to him, he is trained to see the good in you and help you bring it into dominance. He will give you understanding kindliness and will aid you with all the skill at his command.

Many people today are learning to think of a minister in this manner and the results of this newly established relation are encouraging, even amazing. The consultation service has become an integral part of the Protestant ministry. Psychological and psychiatric knowledge is being widely employed. Ministers, of course, do not infringe upon the prerogative of the duly accredited psychologist or psychiatrist, and are exceedingly careful never to go beyond their own knowledge. Ministers are, however, setting apart office hours when members of their church or anyone in the community, for that matter, may come to consult them. Ministers moreover are discussing simple, basic human problems in their sermons with the result that people are becoming increasingly aware that these pastors are truly what their titles indicate: men who understand human beings and who know how to relieve them of their troubles, thus making it possible for them to live effective lives.

Many young ministers nowadays are taking courses with psychiatrists, psychologists and physicians, not that they expect to have medical degrees, for few ministers would desire that, but in order to better understand why people do what they do. Obviously the solution of many problems goes deeper than medication or surgery. Perhaps these pastors are better qualified than those of previous generations to exercise the gifts bestowed by the Great Physician for their scientific knowledge of faith as a therapeutic is probably more extensive.

In some instances ministers have organized a staff in their churches upon which outstanding medical men, psychiatrists, psychologists, and social workers are glad to serve on a clinical basis, or in an advisory capacity.*

In view of this service readily available to modern men and women, it is possible for any person to secure relief and release from the troubles weighing on his mind. So don't keep your troubles to yourself. See a counselor qualified to help you. Go to your minister as you would to a doctor.

I realize that this advice runs counter to a rather common but false heroism. People say, "I always keep my troubles to

----

*In the Marble Collegiate Church on Fifth Avenue, New York City, of which the author is the minister, the eminent psychiatrist, Dr. Smiley Blanton, conducts a clinic in which is assisted by three other psychiatrists, a psychologist, and a social psychiatrist. It is one of the pioneer religio-psychiatric clinics in American churches.

myself." This is usually said with the assumption that such an attitude will be commended. Being close-mouthed about trouble is frequently considered very long-suffering and strong. Under certain circumstances it is commendable and under still other circumstances it is heroic, even inspiring. All of us have known people who have been compelled to suffer pain for years, and who have done so with a glorious spirit, never even allowing pain to show upon their faces. They have not distressed their loved ones and their friends by constant reference to their suffering.

On the other hand, some people seem to develop into whiners and complainers. They are victims of self-pity, thinking constantly about themselves. They do not keep their troubles to themselves and they should learn to do so. They want everybody else to keep their troubles for them, and people do not like to be the repositories of other people's troubles. Ella Wheeler Wilcox well says:

> Laugh, and the world laughs with you;
> Weep, and you weep alone.

But the policy of keeping your troubles to yourself can be dangerous. There is a sense in which the human personality must have release from itself. A person cannot forever bottle up within himself the guilt, the problems and the adversity which have affected him. To use a crude phrase, it is advisable to get some things "off your chest." Perhaps the word "chest" in this common saying is wisely used because it would seem to have reference to the heart. The heart has been traditionally considered the center of emotional life.

In more classic phraseology, Shakespeare gives the same

advice, "Canst thou minister to a mind diseased, pluck from the memory a rooted sorrow, raze out the written troubles of the brain, and by some sweet oblivious antidote cleanse the bosom of the perilous stuff that lies upon the heart?"

Inner release is a necessity faced by every human being. The heart must be relieved. It is a dangerous policy to carry things too long, else they turn inward upon you. So don't keep your troubles to yourself. Get them straightened out by someone who knows the art and is skilled in counseling. People who do follow this suggested procedure, who turn to their minister, their rabbi, or priest, or psychiatrist or psychologist, or other well qualified counselor, or even to some wise and understanding friend, receive profound benefit. Often they receive complete relief from their troubles.

The counselor draws up and out of the mind the ideas and thoughts which have been causing trouble and admits new and healing thoughts. It is impossible to drive out a thought, just by being willing to do so. If by force of will it is ejected momentarily, it comes rushing back into the mind when the pressure is removed or when the guard is down. The only successful and permanent method is to supplant destructive thoughts with good ones, diseased thoughts with healthy ones. To accomplish this the counselor employs specific techniques.

In our interview room a man piteously described his condition. He happened to be a banker in a small city, an influential man in his community. He was a man of unquestioned character and was held in high respect.

"I simply do not understand it," he said. "I live a decent life and try to help people in many ways, but I am unhappy. In fact," he concluded, "I am miserable."

Investigation revealed an inner state of conflict. He was filled with fears and anxieties and there was not a little hate and resentment in his mind. It seemed when we started him to talking that there were more people than even he imagined in his town who irritated him and whom he detested. He had a strong desire to get even but his stern religious training had helped to sublimate much of this antagonism. However, he had not cast it out. He had merely forced it inward where it was creating pressure as steam will when bottled up.

He poured all of this out hesitantly at first, but in a torrential flood as he finally let go of himself and the restraints of embarrassment and self-consciousness were eased.

I listened patiently. The important thing was not what I should advise, but that he should tell everything. In other words, he must get it all out. A complete mental catharsis was required.

How should I advise him? To pray! Yes, but he had been doing that all of his life. To read the Bible! Of course, but daily he had made it a practice to read the Bible. Perfunctory religious words would not suffice. Plainly it was necessary to attack his situation in a simple and yet fresh and original manner. It is my belief that the Christian religion has not been made simple enough, even for educated men of his type. We should learn that the really effective way to make religion a useful tool is to cast it in simple thought forms and work out its techniques in very lucid and simple procedures. It should be made graphic, even picturesque, and a new slant given to lift it out of the dull and lifeless formality which often renders it impotent.

So I said to this man, "Would it not be a fine thing if we could reach down into your mind and take out all of those thoughts which have put your brain into such a turmoil and tumult?"

"You have no idea how wonderful that would be," he declared.

Pursuing the idea, I said, "Wouldn't it be great if a surgeon could take a knife and cut a hole in the top of your head, then take an instrument and go down in and scrape all those ideas out? He might then take one of those instruments such as a dentist uses to blow air into a cavity and blow it all around inside your head to be sure that no vestige of those diseased ideas lurked there. Then when it was all cleaned out, the physician would close up the top of your head."

Then I reminded him of that wise insight in the Bible which says that even if we got the devils out and cleaned the house, they would come trooping back. Therefore it was obvious that he would have to do more than merely to empty his mind and sweep it clean; otherwise the expelled thoughts would, by reason of their long habitat, return and take up their abode in the house which they had been forced temporarily to vacate.

Continuing this rather curious spiritual treatment, I said, "When your head would be all cleaned out, before the physician should close it up, perhaps I as a minister would also be present and I would open the Bible and pick out of it some of those great verses about faith, forgiveness, kindliness, and drop them down into your mind—just cram your brain full of them. Then let the physician close up the hole in the top of your head and clamp it down. Those new ideas in the form of Bible texts would soak into your mind and permeate it, creating a healing influence so that finally you would be changed completely."

He sadly shook his head, laughing as he did so at the oddity of this therapy, and said, "Isn't it too bad that can't be done? It is just a pity."

We sat quietly considering the matter, than I asked, "Why can't it be done?"

"But how?" he demanded. "You can't cut a hole in the top of my head."

"We do not need to do that. There are already two entrances into your brain—your eye and your ear." Therefore my professional advice to you is to go home, take a New Testament, and underline in red every verse that you think you need and commit them one by one to memory. For a time even give up reading books and magazines and only glance at the paper. Concentrate on filling your mind with verses from the Bible. Fully occupy your mind with these healing thoughts so as to prevent the destructive thoughts you have so long harbored from continuing to live in your mind. Concentrate on expelling destructive thoughts by the powerful and creative thoughts taken from the Bible. These words from the Scripture are very powerful and will curette the diseased thoughts out of your mind in due course.

"Then," I said, "go to church and really listen to what is said. Listen beneath your conscious self, eagerly reaching out for vital words and sentences and thoughts. Sincerely meditate upon them and conceive of them as dropping deeply into your brain.

"Thus you will have admitted healing thoughts by the two entrances to your brain which are available to you, namely, your eye and your ear. So the actual hole in your head is not necessary. When you feel a hate thought or a defeat thought coming into your mind, immediately turn to these words and ideas which you have assembled. Say them over quickly. Repeat them again and again. Preserve in this practice and you will soon change the character of your thoughts entirely. Flush out your brain and refill it with healing power."

The banker did as directed. Being a man of considerable mental strength, he was able to apply a simple procedure. Only minds great enough to be simple can benefit by a procedure like this one. Please remember that the greatest of all thinkers, Jesus Christ, said that unless you "become as little children"—you cannot get results.

The banker tells me that as a result of this simple procedure, the whole character of his life is changing, but he warns, "When I let up, those old ideas try to sneak back, but I do not let up and with every passing day I get more and more control. I have found," he concluded, "that by changing my thinking, by putting into my mind the great ideas of my religion, that I can literally force out destructive thoughts. It was a battle at first," he admits, "but the power of faith can overcome any opposition and gradually I am winning the peace of mind which I have sought."

I have found that such simple techniques and procedures often secure extraordinary results. A general contemplation of religion and a formal observance of its forms, while doubtless stimulating and inspiring, is not always sufficient to cure the deep maladies of the soul. The application of specific remedies in some such simple form as suggested in the foregoing incident is often required to bring full relief.

To the reader who may be surprised by the "curious and unusual" procedure recommended to the banker, the best answer is that it worked. It has been my experience, even with the most intellectual and sophisticated persons, that when Christianity is reduced to precise formulas and is applied in simple techniques or devices, it "works" in an amazingly successful manner.

If, as I believe, the minister is a spiritual doctor, he must be in a position to suggest practical spiritual prescriptions.

In counseling, two basic human problems seem constantly to recur. One is fear and the other is guilt. Fear is treated elsewhere in this book, so I shall not discuss it here.

Sin, or a sense of guilt, has a peculiarly damaging effect on the personality. It may be best described as a wound. Guilt cuts deeply into the emotional and spiritual nature. At first this personality cut may not cause suffering and one may feel that "he has got away with it." However, if, like the history of some physical diseases, the development is slow, nevertheless the time comes when this guilt malady begins to cause trouble; all of a sudden it may "break out."

Tension increases, nervousness becomes a problem, curious obsessions develop. One man with whom I worked always had to go back to try the door. Another man washed his hands constantly after touching things. Perhaps like Lady Macbeth, he was trying to wash out a spot which did not exist on his hand but which certainly did exist on his mind. Frequently the obsessions are much deeper and result in acute suffering. The mind becomes unsettled, the emotions are thrown out of gear, and one is desperately unhappy and ineffective.

One cause of this phenomena is that guilt is an unclean wound. Sorrow, for example, is a clean wound. It pains deeply but being clean the would heals according to the process of nature. A clean wound in the flesh heals without difficulty. A tree hit by lightning generally heals over its wound, but the effect of guilt or sin is quite another matter. Being unclean the restorative and curative process cannot be completed. Guilt festers and becomes an infection center; as in the body, so in the mind and the spirit. The personality always and automatically makes the effort to protect itself. Nature strives to isolate an infection center, but in the case of guilt it cannot be done. In youth and even in the strong middle years, its injurious effects may be in part at least halted but with the declining vitality of advancing years and the heavier burden of responsibilities which comes with maturity, resistance declines and the long-held infection of guilt rushes out to dominate the entire system.

Sometimes you hear of men breaking down, having heart trouble, too-high blood pressure, abnormal tension. A vague, unaccountable dissatisfaction tends to spoil their happiness. Not always, of course, is a sense of guilt the root of such difficulties, but in personal counseling we find that it is the cause or at least a contributing factor in a large number of cases.

This particular generation does not seem to like to admit the fact of sin. Some people have gone so far as to say that sin does not exist, but saying so does not make it so. In my opinion one of the profound causes for the nervous tension of this era is that it does not recognize and properly deal with the suppuration of guilt long lodged in human minds. It may also be that the enormous social sins of our time are sapping the mental and emotional health of modern men.

Yes, it is indeed strange and sinister this sense of guilt. You think it won't make any difference and so you take it into your system and presently it begins to throw off what amounts to a "poison," judging by the reaction of the personality. This "poison" gets into your thinking and soon you say to yourself, "I don't seem to be happy. I don't enjoy things any more. I am nervous. Everything has a bad taste. What is the matter with everybody? What is the matter with me?"

Of course, this isn't an actual physical poison but poison is the best word I can think of to describe the unhealthy and deteriorating secretions that flow from a sense of guilt. It has been well established that nervousness or anger or hate can stimulate secretions in the body and disturb the proper functioning of the physical system. Guilt can affect human beings in a similar fashion. Prominent physicians have proven the theory that hate and resentment cause definite physical trouble and there are many laboratory records available in support of these facts. You simply cannot allow the poison of guilt to remain in your mind and at the same time be happy and efficient.

This was illustrated by the case of an officer in the air force who came for an interview. After many missions he was shot down in a raid over some oil fields in Europe. He suffered battle fatigue and shock. He was sent back to a hospital where he was given the splendid treatment which our air force hospitals provided. Still he did not fully recover. Happiness, a grip on life, normal and emotional health eluded him.

Finally the doctor in charge turned him over to the chaplain and through the chaplain he came to our consultation clinic.

In the interviews which followed it came out finally that prior to entering military service, the boy had committed a sex sin. He had attempted to rationalize it on the basis that he was going away and might never see the young lady again. They had planned to be married but circumstances did not permit it at the time and it was hoped that the marriage might take place after the war. However, passing time made both parties feel that it was not wise to consummate the marriage and besides other persons had entered in to complicate the relationship. The boy explained it to himself by a process of rationalization, which is obvious and all too common, but it is a fact that you cannot fool your subconscious mind though you may delude your conscious mind. The mind always tries to save one's face; therefore, the conscious mind is not to be trusted under such circumstances. In the subconscious mind, however, the sin is held and seen for what it is. The mind had attempted to bury it, to isolate it, but it began to fester and finally it was brought out as the cause of the continuing emotional sickness of this young officer.

"Son, your trouble is not in your body," so we told him. "Really it isn't even in your mind. It is in your soul. It is in your moral and spiritual nature." The psychiatrist corroborated the diagnosis.

The boy, being a very alert and intellectually objective young man, recognized the validity of the analysis. He was willing to submit to spiritual treatment, the essence of which was simply that he get the sin forgiven. As soon as he did this (and his attitude was profoundly sincere), the most remarkable change came over him. He quickly became released, happy, even gay, and exuberant. He had such a burst of energy and enthusiasms, that those who knew him were amazed, and no wonder, for a heavy load resting upon his soul had been lifted. Rapidly he returned to health and at the present time is very successful in the job he took after being discharged from the service.

It was difficult at first to persuade the boy to tell the counselor the whole story. This reluctance was not particularly due to a sense of shame, but because he had been led to believe that what we call "sin" no longer has the effect that older generations believed it possessed. His social set had been emphasizing for a large part of his developing years that the thing he did was not really wrong. In fact, he attempted to argue with us that it was not wrong, but nineteen hundred years of Christian civilization had made his subconscious mind know that it is wrong. Therefore his subconscious mind reacted in a manner that was not affected in the slightest by what his particular generation thought about it. Had he followed the beliefs which had been accepted by his conscious mind, he would today be one of those who are wrecked by life. The subconscious is not always your enemy. Indeed it may be your hope as is proved in this case.

In dealing with guilt, the counselor often encounters the strange difficulty that while an individual may feel that he has received the forgiveness of God, he is unable to forgive himself. This is largely due to the fact that the mind has become conditioned to the presence of the guilt complex. There is a curious reluctance in the human mind to let go of guilt no matter how unpleasant. Strange indeed is the mind. It wants freedom and yet hesitates to take freedom when freely offered. It wants to be delivered and yet frequently will not take deliverance when it comes.

I have often noticed that a person who completely confesses guilt and derives the tremendous relief which that confession provides, will presently return and desire to confess the matter all over again and repeatedly.

A man came to see me who confessed a sin and experienced deep relief, but he kept coming back at intervals to confess again the same sin in identical detail. Finally I said to him, "You are having an awfully good time, aren't you?"

"I always feel better after I have confessed this," he replied.

"You may feel better temporarily, but soon your mind begins to take back the guilt. Your mind does not believe that it can be free. It reasons that such deliverance would be too good to be true. Your mind governed by habit is slow to accept the idea that you can be delivered from the domination of the guilt complex. So presently you feel about as badly as you did before you first came to me. But having experienced the release of confession you return to secure once more a temporary peace of mind."

I pointed out to him that he must learn to forgive himself if he expected to break this recurring circle of defeat. In his mind he must forgive himself and take freedom. Instead of the circle which led him from spiritual imprisonment to release and back again, he must walk straight ahead and away, not back around the circle.

I then told him that he must never confess it again to me or to any other person, but on the contrary he must repeatedly say to himself, "Thank God, I am through with that and I intend to remain through with it."

"So," I said to him, "go ahead and confess it to me once more, but this must be the last time it shall ever be spoken."

When he had finished, I said, "Now, that is the last. I will never listen to it again and I strongly urge you never to tell it to another person." I felt sure he would not confess to another because he had a hard enough time telling me the first time. I had become a kind of spiritual father to him, a releasing agent, but if he was to be cured, he had to make a transference beyond me to God and to his own mind. He had to accept forgiveness from both God and himself. Repeated confession indicated he had not really surrendered his guilt.

It was several months before I found his name again on my appointment book. When I entered the interview room, he stood up and with a vigor I had never previously noticed about him, he literally crushed my hand with his handclasp.

"Well, my friend, what is on your mind this time?" I asked.

Quickly he replied. "Don't you worry. I am not going to confess that matter again. I just came in to tell you that at last I am through with it. I only want to tell you that the very minute I decided the whole matter was finally cleared up, that God truly had forgiven me, then I did as you suggested, I forgave myself and at last I walked away from it. It seemed to drop away and I actually have left it behind."

Then he added, "I have committed to memory that passage of Scripture that you gave me and what a wonderful thing it is. It really works: at any rate, it has for me."

The passage from the Bible which I gave him is this, "Forgetting those things which are behind and reaching forth unto those things which are before, I press toward..." (Philippians 3:13-14.) So, don't keep your troubles to yourself. But once having told them to a competent counselor and been forgiven by God, and having found release, then forgive yourself and turn your back definitely on them. Fill your mind with hopeful, helpful and positive thoughts. Have faith and go forward. Don't look back. March straight ahead for always life lies straight ahead—never backward. Press forward.

Once in my counseling work I had a unique experience in this connection. A little, white-haired old lady came to see me. She was obviously under great distress. She had a very sweet face, one not unlike Whistler's immortal portrait of a mother. As the series of interviews progressed, I found myself more and more drawn to the conclusion that it was a guilt case. It seemed unlikely in view of the gentleness and beauty of her personality, yet I realized that a competent physician of the soul must explore every possibility. Therefore with exceeding diffidence I raised the question whether in her experience she had acquired a sense of guilt, whether she had committed a sin, or, what is more subtle, whether she thought she had done so.

It turned out that the last was the answer to the problem. She related that as a young girl of about eighteen years of age she had been very much in love. She had been raised in a strict Christian home and her ideals of personal conduct and personal purity were very high. The young man with whom she was in love was a bit more flexible in his morality and it seems that they verged on the commission of a sex sin. His insistence to yield to his false moral reasoning was considerable. She assured me however that she did not yield to him but, she said, "Here is the terrible thing about it—I desired to do so. It was only after the most awful battle with myself that I was able to resist it."

Now, she said, "I read in the Bible 'That whosoever looketh on a woman to lust after her hath committed adultery with her already in his heart.' So I saw at once my guilt.

I had not performed this act, but it had been my desire, therefore I was just as guilty as if I had done so. All my life long," she concluded, "I have lived a clean righteous life, but in this I sinned and it has haunted me and I know that when I die, I will be damned," so concluded her pathetic story.

I pointed out to her that we cannot govern the thoughts that come into our minds. In the words of an old saying, "You cannot keep the birds from flying over your head, but you can keep them from building nests in your hair." I explained that actually what she had done was to achieve a great moral and spiritual victory. I told her that she had met the enemy on the battlefield of her life and after a terrible battle had destroyed him and that rather than condemn herself she should thank God that she had the inner strength to win this struggle. But it was to no avail. The idea of guilt so long held could not be that easily dissipated.

Finally I did something which is perhaps not regular in Protestant practice, but it was effective. I asked her to remove her hat and I had her kneel at the altar of the church. Standing behind the altar, I said to her, "You recognize me, do you not, as a minister of the Church?"

She said, "Yes."

"As a minister of the Church, do I stand as a human representative to you of God?"

"Yes," she said, "you do."

"Do you believe that God will forgive you of any wrong and take the burden of any guilt off your mind, and do you now confess your wrongdoing and trust in Jesus Christ as your Savior?"

"Yes," she said, "I sincerely believe, and I do put my faith in Christ."

I then laid my hand upon her head. I was touched by this and I can yet remember my hand resting upon her snowy white hair. She was at least seventy-five years old, perhaps as good a woman as ever walked the earth, a saint though she did not know it. I then said to her, "In the name of Jesus Christ, who alone can forgive sins, I declare that by His power you are forgiven for any wrong. Go and sin no more," and I added, "Forgetting those things which are behind, and reaching forth unto those things which are before, I press toward..."

After a moment or two of quiet prayer, she stood up and looked at me. I have often seen glory on human faces but never more resplendent that that on her face. "I feel so happy. I think it is gone," she said simply.

She lived for four years after that and several times she said to me, "Why didn't I go to somebody long years ago and have that thing taken away?"

She learned the value of not keeping her troubles to herself. She found that anyone can be released from his troubles.

Chapter Three

HOW TO GET RID OF YOUR INFERIORITY COMPLEX

"There is enough atomic energy in the body of one man to destroy the city of New York," says a prominent physicist. We read these words with surface understanding but let us try to press them deep into our minds and realize them. There is enough power in *you* to blow the city of New York to rubble. That, and nothing less, is what advanced physics tells us.

That being so, and it is undeniable, why have an inferiority complex? If there is literally enough force in you to blow up the greatest city in the world, there is also literally enough power in you to overcome every obstacle in your life.

Pythagoras was absolutely right. "Know yourself," he urged. That includes knowing your powers. When you do know yourself and realize tremendous power within yourself, you will then know that you do not need to be a defeated person—defeated because you are beset by a false feeling of inferiority.

Quite possibly you often do feel defeated. Depression settles over you, bringing the disheartening feeling that there isn't much use in fighting on. Probably everybody is tempted to sink into this dull and gloomy attitude occasionally, but not everybody yields to it. Those who accept the idea that they are defeated usually *are* beaten; for, as a famous psychologist says, "There is a deep tendency in human nature to become like that which you imagine yourself to be." Believe you are defeated, believe it long enough, and it is likely to become a fact—even though "there is enough atomic energy in the body of one man to destroy the city of New York."

But notice: people who achieve happiness and success are those who when they tend to sink into a depressed mood shake it off by refusing to accept the idea of defeat. They refuse to entertain the thought that situations and circumstances, or their enemies, have them down. They know it is the *thought* of defeat that causes defeat, so they practice thinking positive thoughts. Indomitable thoughts, thoughts of faith surge through their minds. They train their minds to think victory. As a result they gain victory.

Basically the inferiority complex—habitually feeling inferior to others—arises from wrong thinking acquired either in childhood or as a result of later experiences. An inferiority complex may be defined as a system of emotionally toned ideas ranged around one central idea—disbelief in one's self.

Symptoms of an inferiority complex may be recognized by the way you tend to compensate; that is, by the method your subconscious mind uses to make up for inferiority feelings. If we look briefly at certain types of compensation, we shall gain a comprehensive idea of how disbelief in one's self influences human behavior.

There is the type of personality which over-asserts itself. The victim instead of walking, struts. He is pompous. When he talks it is likely to be in a loud voice. When he discusses any subject, he gives the impression of knowing all there is to know. You say, "How conceited he is!" Not necessarily. It might be more accurate to say, "How sick he is." Beneath his pompous assertiveness he has a profound feeling of inadequacy. His overbearing attitude is the way his mind unconsciously seeks to make up for the inferiority feeling. He is not deliberately or consciously doing this. It is the unconscious effort of his mind to save face. It is his subconscious mind over-asserting itself.

In contrast, but from the same cause, there is the under-assertive type. For example, you sometimes meet a man on the links who plays golf very well, but always acts supermodest. He says, "I would like to play, but I'm out of practice and am poor at best, I'm not at all a good golfer." To get him to play you have to coax him. The queer twist here is that the man is egotistic over his humility. A normal person will say, "Sure, I'll be glad to play," and will play the best game he can with relaxed naturalness.

Still another form of compensation is that in which a person manifests an inferiority complex by an infantile reaction.

Years ago I worked in a newspaper office in a certain city where I encountered a woman who illustrated this type. She came bristling into the newspaper and actually complained because she did not get her picture in the paper in connection with a society function. After she left the office the city editor said, "I don't understand that woman." That isn't all he said, but that is the part that is printable. At the time I did not understand her, either, but I think I do now. As a baby every time she dropped her rattle, somebody rescued it at once. When she cried for anything she got it. When she became an adult she expected the world to continue to baby her. She is still essentially a baby, with a strong sense of inadequacy. She retreats into an infantile manifestation of inferiority.

The inferiority complex sometimes takes a curious turn. A deep inner feeling of inadequacy may manifest itself in an unreasonable desired to dominate. A person who in infancy was over-dominated may in adult life over-compensate by himself seeking to dominate others. This person may not, indeed, usually does not, recognize this cause of his own attitudes, nor do others with whom he is associated. In any abnormal emotional situation, among other possible causes that of hidden inferiority may wisely be explored.

A woman came to interview me because, as she put it, she "could hardly live any more."

"I am surrounded," she complained, "by people who are constantly in turmoil. I must have peace or I'll go mad."

Her home, she said, was "bedlam"—in upheaval all the time. Everybody in her house was nervous—it was a high-strung, tense household. "Why," she fumed, "it's just awful." She said she was so high-strung she couldn't sleep. In short, she declared, an intolerable situation.

I asked her to bring her husband to see me, thinking perhaps he might be the cause of this turmoil, but he proved to be a meek, mild-mannered little man. He sat quietly while she did all the talking. Obviously he was a defeated personality. He would even look apprehensively at her before speaking, then speaking timorously.

I decided to persuade the members of the family to go away from home one after the other, calculating that if the turmoil ceased in the absence of any one of them, the one who went away was, by a process of elimination, the cause of the upheaval. That seemed a simple way to work things out.

The children went away first, one after the other; then the husband went off, but nothing happened to change the situation, which remained as tumultuous as ever.

Finally I asked the wife to go away for a while.

"Well," she replied, "I don't think that will solve it. If I go away, who will take care of the place?"

"Never mind that," I said. "You just go away. How long have you been married?" She told me, and I said, "Any wife who has been married that long deserves a vacation. Go away somewhere for two weeks."

She went away for a fortnight. When she left home everything calmed down. It became quiet and peaceful. Although some of the household tasks were not done efficiently, it was a place of peace and quiet.

"How are things?" I asked the husband.

He whispered, "Wonderful—great." Looking furtively about, he confided, "Everything is marvelous."

After two weeks the wife returned and came in with her husband to talk with me. I said, "We have made an experiment. We sent the three children away one by one and nothing happened. We sent the husband away; nothing happened. We sent the wife away and everything became peaceful."

"Yes," she admitted, "that's what they say." After pondering for a moment, she asked reflectively, "You don't suppose I could be the cause of it, do you?"

At this her husband came to life with magnificent assertiveness and said, "Yes, Mary, you are the cause."

She turned to him and snapped, "You keep out of this—I'll decide for myself."

"What is my trouble?" she asked.

I liked her; she was honest. She knew the fault lay within herself, and she wanted the answer. When the mechanism of inferiority was described in the light of her reactions, she recognized the accuracy of the diagnosis. She was unconsciously over-compensating for domination she had suffered in childhood. Her mind took this method of trying to escape from a deep inferiority feeling.

She asked for guidance in correcting her personality faults. A definite and detailed plan of spiritual technique was outlined for her. She was a forthright character, and she put it into practice, with the result that the situation was completely rectified.

One day she wisely observed, "Perhaps the best way to change a situation is to change yourself."

Know yourself—change yourself—that is very important. But there is an even deeper factor in eradicating inferiority, and it is to be found among the vast psychological riches of the Bible. Among the possible methods, one of the best and surest is the formula contained in the words, "If God be for us, who can be against us?" (Romans 8:31.)

That formula has incalculable potency. If you believe what those words imply, you will develop faith in your own powers. Furthermore, you will discover that faith releases forces which come powerfully to your aid.

Let me give you a graphic illustration of the manner in which this formula works.

In Cedar Rapids, Iowa, I met Arthur Poe, one of the famous six Poe brothers who played football at Princeton around the turn of the century. The Poes are probably the most famous football family in American athletic history, for all six of the brothers were stars of the first magnitude.

That night in my speech in Cedar Rapids, I emphasized at some length the power of positive thinking, and asserted that practice of the techniques of faith makes it possible for a person to overcome difficulties. Positive thinking was outlined as a cure for the inferiority complex.

After the meeting a man introduced himself as Arthur Poe. He said, "You are right about the power of positive thought, and my own experience has proven to me conclusively what real faith can do. Without it I would have had a terrible inferiority complex."

When he went up to Princeton as Poe Number Five, having been preceded by four great football brothers, he, too, wanted to carry on the family tradition. He went out for football and made the freshman team. But late in the season he suffered a very severe injury to his leg. The doctors told him that he would never again be able to play football. Naturally, he was heartbroken. Throughout the winter and summer he nursed his leg, but the verdict held that he was through with football.

Finally, at his mother's suggestion, Poe adopted the mental attitude of putting the matter of his injured leg in the hands of God. He developed the capacity and skill of having faith. He practiced mentally accepting the formula, "If God be for us, who can be against us?"

"As a result," he said, "I played football at Princeton."

I looked up the athletic record of Arthur Poe at Princeton, and found that when he said, "I played football at Princeton," he was engaging in magnificent understatement. He did play, and with such brilliance that the memory of his athletic exploits still has the power to thrill old Princetonians, and others of a later generation who hear the story.

It was November 12, 1898. The big Princeton-Yale game was in progress. No score had been made. Princeton was being forced back toward its own goal line. Yale, marching down the field, apparently could not be stopped. But Durston of Yale fumbled; and a boy whom they said could never again play football scooped up the ball. Shaking off Yale tacklers, he started to run. He forgot about his leg. He ran like a sprinter. Down the field he went as fleet as a deer—thrilling, inspiring. Ninety-five yards, the length of the field, he ran, crossing the goal line ten feet ahead of the nearest Yale man. Arthur Poe, running on a leg that was supposed to be incapacitated, beat Yale singlehanded. The final score was 6-0.

On November 25, 1899, Yale and Princeton were again battling for supremacy. It was the last thirty seconds of play. Suddenly the ball shot in the hands of Arthur Poe. He fell back as if to kick, but nobody expected him to kick, for with that bad leg he had never before attempted it. Everybody expected him to run, but he did not have time to run. It was kick or nothing. Arthur Poe drew back, dropped the ball; his toe caught it, and in a beautiful arc it sailed across the goal post, touching the ground just as the whistle blew, and Princeton won by a single point.

Arthur Poe did not tell me this story. When I read the account I have just summarized, I remembered the conviction in his voice as he said that all his life long he had practiced the principle that a man can overcome any obstacle by a simple faith in God.

How easy it would have been for young Poe to have developed an inferiority complex! He could easily have been thwarted in his ambition to play football, and, what is worse, he could have gone through life defeated by an inner sense of inadequacy. He refused to accept an inferiority complex. Arthur Poe got rid of it before it took root by the simple expedient of intelligently employing his religious faith.

The victim of the inferiority complex always tends to think he is defeated. Thinking so helps to produce that outcome. But the mental attitude of putting up a fight gets results, especially when you have developed and regularly practiced the thought pattern that you have an invincible ally. Say it this way, "If God be for me, who can be against me?"

Do you recall the immortal and ancient parable of the two frogs who fell into a jar of cream? The top of the cream was quite a distance from the opening of the jar. The frogs tried to leap out, but could not make it. They struggled, they stewed, they fretted, they did everything possible to get out, all without success.

Finally one frog assumed a negative attitude. He began to think defeat thoughts, and the acids of futility stated to spread through his mind. He became a pessimist. He said to himself, "I know I can't get out of this jar of cream, so why should I wear myself out trying?" I have to die, anyway, so why not get it over; why not die in peace?" In despair and resignation he sank into the cream and died. His epitaph was, "He died of an inferiority complex."

The other frog was made of sterner stuff. He had a different training and background and evidently came of a long line of dauntless frogs. He was a positive thinker. He said to himself, "Sure, I may die, but if I do I shall go down with every flag flying. But I shall fight my way out of this if it is humanly [I suppose that should be "froggily"] possible; and if in the end I can't make it, I shall die proudly in the glorious tradition of the ancient and honorable frogs."

With this he went at it with all his vigor. He swam around, he thrashed about, he beat the cream and made a great stir. As a result, gradually he began to feel solid footing under him and his activity churned the cream into butter. Finally his legs, whipping like little pistons, got traction, and he leaped victoriously from the jar, the contents of which had now turned into solid butter.

Religious faith puts fight into a man so that he develops a terrific resistance to defeat. Obstacles no longer awe him. He uses obstacles as stepping stones to cross over from failure to success.

Fortitude and faith are the words. That is what keeps a man going when he seems defeated. Believe that if you put your trust in God and keep at things with unremitting energy and intelligence you, too, can build a solid foundation beneath you upon which you may mount up to victory. Therefore, train your mind never to accept the thought of defeat about anything. That verse from the Bible makes an unbeatable inspiration in any situation: "If God be for us, who can be against us?" Hold it habitually in mind and it will train you to believe in yourself by constantly reminding you that you have extra power available.

I have put a religious slant into the curing of inferiority for one reason only: *Christianity is entirely practical.* It is astounding how defeated persons can be changed into victorious individuals when they actually utilize their religious faith as a workable instrument. I am so sure of this that I unhesitatingly assert that I have never seen anything that can really down a person and keep him down if that person definitely and intelligently practices his faith. There is no situation which I have ever seen—and as a minister I've seen plenty—in which faith in God will not help.

In a hard spot, practice saying over and over to yourself, making the statement personal, "If God be for *me*, who can be against *me*?" This practice will eventually cause acceptance by your mind of the powerful thought that your inadequacy is relieved by greater force. Practice saying this formula and keep on saying it; perserverance will get results. Faith is a vital medium for recreating strength, hope and efficiency. It has a strange therapeutic and recreative effect. I could cite many cases in support of the preceding sentence, but the following incident is typical of them all.

A soldier came home from overseas minus a leg. The amputation following battle wounds shocked the boy's mind deeply. He lay on his bed neither smiling nor speaking—just starting at the ceiling. He would not cooperate in learning to wear an artificial limb, although others around him were doing so. Obviously his problem was not his physical body but was in his mind and spirit. So deep was his acquired inferiority that he had completely given way to defeat.

It was thought that a period of time at his own home might help bring him out of himself and assist in lifting his depression. He came of a well-to-do family, and at home he had every attention. In fact, his family overdid it. He was tenderly lifted into his bath, he was hovered over and coddled in every conceivable manner. This is understandable, for everybody wants to show love and appreciation for a boy who has sacrificed himself for his country.

However, the doctor realized that they were making a permanent invalid of the boy. Accordingly he placed him in a convalescent hospital. An effort was made to help him to help himself, and to give him a normal attitude toward the problem of himself but with no success. He continued to lie on his bed, indifferent and uncooperative.

One day the rather baffled and exasperated young doctor said, "I have got to be hard on the boy; I hate to do it, but somehow I must break through this wall around him. He must cast out this inferiority psychosis if he is to recover to normal living."

He said, "Soldier, we are not going to pamper you any more, or carry you around. You have got to be awakened, boy. We can do nothing for you until you open that mind of yours. We all feel sorry about that leg, but other men have lost legs in battle and they have carried on with good spirit. Besides, a man can live and be happy and have a successful career without a leg or an arm or an eye." The doctor pointed out how people are able to adjust themselves, and how so many have done astounding things.

This talk did not move the boy in the slightest. Finally, after many days of attempting to open the closed mind of his patient the doctor quite unconsciously did a peculiar thing, something which amazed even himself.

The doctor was not a particularly religious person, and up to this point had seldom, if ever, mentioned religion in his practice. However, this day in sheer desperation the doctor literally shouted at the boy. "All right, all right; if you won't let any of us help you—if you are so stubborn that you won't even help yourself—then, then—why don't you let God help you? Get up and get that leg on; you know how to do it."

With this he left the room.

A few hours later it was reported that the boy was up, had on his artificial leg, and was moving around. The doctor said that one of the most thrilling moments in his medical experience came some days later when he saw this boy walking around the grounds with a girl friend.

Later when the soldier was discharged from the hospital he came in to see the doctor. The physician started to give him some suggestion, but the boy said "It's all right, Doc; I remember the medicine you gave me that day. And I think with that prescription I can get along well enough."

"What prescription?" asked the doctor.

"Don't you remember the day you told me that if I could not do it myself, to let God help me? Well, that did something to me. I felt sort of different inside, and as I thought about it, it began to come over me that maybe I could do it—that maybe I wasn't finished after all."

As the physician related this story he sat tapping his desk with a pencil in a thoughtful manner. "Whatever happened to that boy I cannot explain; the process eludes my knowledge. But I do know that in some spiritual manner that boy was released. His mind changed from a state of inner defeat to one of personal power." He hesitated, then added, "There seems to be a very great power in religious faith when it is practiced."

And he is right. Use your religious faith and you do not need to be a defeated person. It will recondition your mind from negative to positive reactions. It makes possible what formerly seemed impossible. This is the mechanism which explains the Biblical statement, "With men things are impossible, but with God all things are possible." When you mentally live with thoughts of God, your inferiority changes to power, impossibility changes to possibility.

In fact, that brief statement of ten short words from the Bible which I have quoted several times can absolutely revolutionize your life. "If God be for us, who can be against us?" Strong, sturdy words these. With these ten words of power you can stand up against any human situation and not be defeated.

In ridding oneself of an inferiority complex, the techniques at hand should not be underrated because they are simple. The purpose is to change the thought slant. Inferiority is a malady of the thoughts, and any device, however simple, that changes the pattern of thinking may be employed.

A young man came to see me who said he was having a nervous breakdown. He did not look it; he was a vigorous, healthy person. He was a bit on edge, however, and obviously high-strung. He was not having a nervous breakdown, but was trying to imagine himself into one. He sat in my office reciting one by one the "enormous" difficulties he was then experiencing. I made a few suggestions of an optimistic character, but he immediately leaped upon them and began to tell why they couldn't be done. He was expert in advancing objections. He was what I once heard a businessman refer to as an "obstacle man"—a man adept in finding obstacles. He leaped on these suggestions of mine with such vigor and alacrity, such condemnatory skill, that he almost convinced me that everything *was* against him.

Finally, I said to him: "It is a shame that life is treating you so badly and that you are a failure. It is too bad, too, that you are breaking down and going to pieces; I feel very sorry for you."

He looked at me in amazement, and then he all but got out of his chair; he sat on the edge of it. There was a flash in his eyes and a flush on his face. His whole manner became aggressive.

"I am not a failure," he snapped. He threw back his head with the air of saying, "I can do things."

Indeed, he then did everything but call me names, and I looked admiringly at him and said, "Wonderful! That's wonderful!"

"If you would get up each morning and talk to yourself in the mirror just as you are talking now," I advised, "you would convince yourself that you have strength and power and possibilities within you." I actually urged him to stand before a mirror and talk to himself in just that fashion, and to say out loud the ten tremendous words, "If God be for us, who can be against us?"

He actually did just that! His wife told me she was never so amazed as to her big, strapping husband talking with himself in the bedroom, standing before a mirror saying to himself, "You can do things. You have brains. God is with you. If God be for you, who can be against you?" She walked in on him and found him thus, to his embarrassment.

That man now has a grip on himself. When I meet him, as I do occasionally, he says, "It is all due to a text—yes, a text." While the text helped, of course, so had the simple procedure which he practiced. It was designed to get his mind to thinking the idea contained in the Bible text.

It works when you believe it—and practice it. He learned the secret of driving off his inferiority complex by employing a practical formula.

The simple but effective technique of faith described above is greatly needed today, for everywhere human beings are afflicted with the inferiority complex. The feeling of inadequacy or inferiority is a widespread deterrent in personality development. It may well be that the rise of inferiority of a personality problem is due to the decline of religion among the people. If there is a connection between the decline of religion and the prevalence of inferiority, then the remedy is plain: revive religious faith and inferiority feelings will diminish. The spiritual principles suggested here are not theoretical. It is a proven fact, demonstrated in case after case, that religious faith properly applied can rid people of the inferiority complex.

Those ten words from the Bible contain the basic solution to the inferiority complex. They represent one of the greatest, if not the greatest, spiritual and psychological facts in releasing personality; namely, the thought of God's presence with *you*. Practice believing that God is with you and you will get to believing that nothing *can* be against you. By a subconscious procedure the sense of inferiority and inadequacy gradually give way to one of confidence and faith.

Fear and faith, as previously pointed out, are the two greatest powers competing for control of the human mind. Inferiority and inadequacy on the one side; faith and effectiveness on the other—that is the issue. But never forget that faith is stronger than fear; adequacy is stronger than inadequacy.

Repeat those ten words of reassurance a half-dozen times every day; let them saturate your mind. When you face a critical or difficult situation, practice saying to yourself, "God is with me; I can meet the crisis that I now face."

I have a friend, a successful businessman named Jerry Henderson, who practices this technique, and I am indebted to him for a very striking story of its efficiency. You will see by this story that I have not made exaggerated claims.

Henderson was in the Canadian Rockies at Lake Louise to climb and to ski with a party of friends. Shortly before, one of the most famous ski masters had been killed in a heavy avalanche and the suggestion of danger was potent.

Henderson's party went with their guide to climb White Eagle peak. They climbed all morning, and by noontime had surmounted five thousand of the nine thousand feet they had set out to climb. At this point the guide told them that they had to cross a transverse valley lying before them. The sides shot down at an angle of forty-five to fifty degrees.

"Do not call or whistle or raise your voices, for it might start an avalanche," the guide warned. Since hearing of the death of the ski master all had been impressed by the danger of avalanches.

The guide took from his pack a big ball of red yarn. He cut off fifty-foot lengths and gave to each one.

"Tie this around your waist," he said, "If an avalanche starts, shake off your skis, throw away your poles and start swimming just as if you were in the water. This will tend to bring you to the top. If the avalanche buries you, the end of this red yarn will protrude and we can find you."

In the party was a girl in her twenties. She looked down at this steep declivity and thought of the possibility of an avalanche, and she became very frightened. She began to whimper and cry, and said to Jerry Henderson, "I can't do it. I'm terrified. I simply can't do it."

He did not feel any too blithe about it himself, but Henderson believes in and practices the ten great words. He takes the position that one need not fear if God is with him; that one can reasonably count on God to see him through whatever comes.

He turned to the trembling, hysterical girl and said quietly, "The Lord has watched over you throughout your life, hasn't he? You believe that, do you not?"

"Yes," she sobbed.

"Well, then, can't you trust Him to take care of you for the next twenty minutes?" he asked.

A remarkable change came over the girl. She made the descent beautifully, taking her place in the long graceful line as each skier followed the other about forty yards apart. She made the descent with exultation. She had achieved a marvelous sense of victory over herself. She learned that there is a secret through which one can get rid of his inferiority complex.

Try simple religious practices. They work. You can be rid of your inferiority complex.

Chapter Four

HOW TO ACHIEVE A CALM CENTER
FOR YOUR LIFE

High tension is a prevailing American malady. The adult who has not apprehensively watched the doctor take his blood pressure is in the minority. Glance at the obiturary columns of the daily papers, and note how often the cause of death is high blood pressure, angina pectoris, and other hypertension afflictions. Many "strokes" have excessive tension as a contributing, if not a root, cause. For multitudes of high-strung, nervous people life is constant and unrelieved strain.

A well-known physician says: "American business and professional men are not living out their normal life expectancies. The tension and pressure of these troublous times, the pace of American life, worry, and uncertainty, are wreaking havoc among these men of forty and more. They are dying altogether too soon.

"Heart disease, high blood pressure and arterial disease, kidney disease, nervous disorders, cancer, gastro-intestinal troubles—these are the worst enemies of America's men of responsibility and leadership. Note that few of these are germ-caused diseases; they fall into the classification of 'degenerative diseases.'

"We know how to control the germ-caused diseases: typhoid, scarlet fever, diptheria, smallpox, and tuberculosis. But the degenerative diseases which come about because of the age of the individual plus wrong living habits, too much work, strain, stress, too little rest and relaxation, are the troubles which are mowing down so many of our valuable people forty years of age or more

"Worry, fear, strain, overwork, under-rest, excesses in sex, nicotine and alcohol, wrong diet, overweight; all may bring your blood pressure to dangerous heights. Twenty-five percent of all deaths of those men over 50 years of age are due to hypertension."*

Apparently Americans have always been more or less of this tense type. A French writer came to this country in 1830 to study the American, whom he classified as a "a new breed of man on the earth." The French visitor noted the restless aggressiveness of our people.

"The American," he complained, "is so restless that he has even invented a chair, calling a rocking chair, in which he can move while he sits."

If this French observer could see us now he would surely be forced to revise upward his conclusion, as the tempo has mounted.

A Scotch physician analyzes us. "You Americans," he concludes, "wear too much expression on your faces. You are living with all your nerves in action."

Sometimes our worry over our national tenseness takes a grotesque form...Two women were overhead in a Florida city talking about their troubles, consisting mainly of bad hearts and high blood pressure. It seems that men go about

---

*M. A. Mortenson, M.D., in *Battle Creek Sanitarium News*, Vol. 13, No. 3.

the streets of this city with blood pressure instruments and do quite a business.

One woman asked, "Did you have that man down on blank street take your blood pressure?"

No, indeed, I did not. He charges 25¢. I had mine taken by the man up on the other street who only charges 15¢," replied the other woman.

A primary factor in tension is mental disorganization. The helter-skelter mind always feels overburdened. A disorderly mental state means confusion and, of course, tension. Such a mind rests lightly upon problems which it never decides. It skips nervously from one presented problem to another, never arriving at a settled conclusion, in fact, not even grappling seriously with the issue involved. Thus deferred decisions accumulate. The result? The mind gives up and cries desperately, "I am swamped"—simply because it is not organized. It is cluttered up and *seems*, therefore, to be overwhelmed. Note the emphasis, *seems*.

The mind in this situation reacts somewhat like the body in shivering. One shivers when passing suddenly from a warm to a cold area; the body attempts to accommodate itself quickly to the sudden change in body temperature. It has been estimated that as much energy is expended in a half-minute of shivering as in several hours of work. This results in depletion of vigor. In a similar way, shivering in the mind depletes its force when one fails to practice the fundamental principle of mental organization.

Get the calm selective ability to take up one thing at a time and concentrate upon it. Deal finally with it, if possible, before passing to the next matter.

In my office we receive a heavy daily mail covering a wide variety of matters. We operate on the policy that every letter gets an answer. I used to come to my office and find a formidable pile of letters—and be dismayed. Contemplating the labor of thinking out replies to those letters, my mind would inwardly (and sometimes outwardly) complain, "Oh my, oh my, how can I ever get these letters answered?" It was the "I am swamped" reaction. But I learned that the way to answer letters is to answer them as they arrive. A letter unanswered for two weeks has answered itself.

There is only one way to work down a pile of letters. Pick up the first letter, decide upon an answer, and dictate that answer at once. If information not immediately obtainable is required, dictate a memorandum pertaining to it and put the letter in the proper receptacle. If additional study is indicated, place it in a receptacle for pending matters—but don't let them "pend" too long. Handle the letter in some way. Do not put it down indecisively, only to pick it up aimlessly again and again. If you follow this ineffective course, the letters will pile up until your desk is a nightmare, and your mind will fight back with the cry. "I can't stand it—this strain is too much." Then your mind will tell you that you are unequal to your job, and if you keep at this procedure too long you may have a nervous breakdown.

When you organize your mind, a sense of power will come to you, and you will soon wonder at the ease with which you can handle responsibilities. Your capacity for work will increase; so will your pleasure in what you are doing. Strain and tension will subside.

A careful and consistent cultivation of a relaxed mental attitude is important in reducing tension. Americans are inheritors of the Horatio Alger tradition: "strive and succeed." The author is an apostle of hard work, of the good old American principle of creating your own wealth and position by means of your own abilities and efforts. But there is a sense in which it is a mistake to try too hard. Effortless ease is the procedure best designed to achieve superior results with the least strain. Athletes know that trying too hard throws them off their timing. The fine coordination which characterizes the great men of sport is attained by the principle of "taking the game in stride." They do not go into the game to make a record, or get the headlines, or to become stars. They play the game for the love of it. They are alert, they think of the team rather than themselves. They play the game with naturalness and so to the full extent of their ability.

The sports writer, Grantland Rice, reports a conversation with Joe Gordon, then of the New York Yankees, in which the famous player told of an experience in World Series baseball. In his first World Series, Gordon said he was "tied up" all the time. "I wanted to make a great record and hit the headlines. As a result I became tense and rigid and did poorly." In the next series Joe Gordon was wiser. He decided to forget he was playing in a World Series. He determined instead to play ball just as he had on the sand lots, "because it is the grandest game in the world," and to have a good time playing. This released the tension in his mind, and therefore in his nerves and muscles. He became a natural player. As a result he made a much better record in the second series; in fact, he was one of the stars.

In a World Series game, "Dizzy" Trout was on the mound for the Detroit Tigers. He wore glasses. He had been ill and without practice for two weeks; and it was so damp before the game that he couldn't limber up his muscles and get relaxed. And yet he had to go into a World Series game before 42,000 fans in a hostile city and pitch. That demanded calmness, and he had his own way of securing it.

When things got tense, as they did quite often, he simply took off his glasses and wiped them painstakingly, while 42,000 people watched expectantly and the batter at the plate fidgeted. Then he put on his glasses, and began pitching, and one by one the Cubs struck out.

There's calmness for you! Some wag remarked that all of the Chicago Cubs would wear spectacles the next season.

Whatever your work may be—writing books, teaching children, running a business, cooking for a family, working in a factory, plowing a field, or preaching sermons—give your job your best; work hard, slight nothing, take everything in your stride; stay relaxed. Don't try too hard for effect; do not strain for success. Do your job naturally, because you like it, and success will take care of itself.

I learned this basic truth from a red cap in a Chicago station. I was on my way to speak in a city in Western Illinois, and had three "important" calls to make in Chicago between trains, but my train from New York got later and later. I paced the corridor and fumed and fretted. I worked myself into a fair-sized dither. Finally the train rolled into the grimy, cavernous terminal. Will ill-concealed impatience I waited for the porter to get the bags onto the station platform. I was the first man off, and luckily secured a porter, as I had two heavy bags.

"Please bring those bags quickly," I directed. "I am in a terrible hurry."

I started at high speed down the platform. Conscious that he was not following, I turned impatiently. "Come on, I'm late." But there stood the porter calmly looking at me.

"Where you steamin' for, brother?" he asked me. "That ain't no way to make time." Then he said, "Just walk on ahead and I'll come along, and there won't be two minutes between us." I slowed down as admonished and walked along beside his truck. He turned and gave me one of those big smiles with which colored men are blessed, and said, "I'se livin' de relaxed life... Take it easy, boss," he advised. "You can do a lot in a short time if you just go along easy at it. Besides," he concluded, "you'll live longer."

"Thanks, my friend," I said, rather humbly. "I happen to be a minister, and I will preach this idea to my congregation. Do you go to church?"

"Yes, indeed, suh, I sure does; and" (here he finished me completely) "I tries to practice what I hear there."

So I slowed down, made my calls, and had time to spare, but I was tired before I got started. Much of the energy needed for the day had been nervously dissipated by tension. Relaxation is best secured by remembering that "Easy does it." Practice using the light touch and you will be surprised to find that success comes easily.

It is important to maintain a constant intake of energy. A National War Fitness Conference held during World War II days was attended by educators and representatives of the armed services who came together to discuss recreation. The value of games and calisthenics was emphasized, but the conference surprisingly declared that the best recreation is to go to church. Recreation means *re-creation*, they explained.

By going to church and practicing the technique of spiritual living, one can establish contact with the basic flow of energy which we call God's power. The New Testament says, "In Him we live, and move, and have our being." This means that God does not create a man and then abandon him to get along as best he can on his own. He makes it possible for constant re-creation or renewal to take place. By utilizing methods of contacts which are known to be effective, spiritual energy renews power in the soul, the mind, and the body. The electric clock is automatically rewound by the current flowing through the universe. In similar manner people are revitalized who maintain a close spiritual contact. It is the natural way to live.

Mrs. Thomas A. Edison described her husband to me as "Nature's man." He could work long and hard," she said, "then lie on his old couch and immediately go to sleep. He would relax completely and sleep soundly. When he awakened he was instantly wide awake and refreshed."

The inventor did not find it necessary to woo sleep or to fight his way back to an awakening. Thomas Edison seemed to be carried along by some flow of power.

"Never," said Mrs. Edison, "was there any disunity of mind, never obsessions or impeded flow of energy. He was like a child in God's hands; Nature's man. perhaps this was one reason God could pour all those wonderful ideas through his mind."

It appears that the wizard of Menlo Park was in harmony with the universe, and therefore the secret places were unlocked for him. Edison "lived and moved and had his being" in the source of never-failing energy and adjusted personality.

The thought that a human being can sensitize and tune his personality so that he can be the beneficiary of an automatic renewal of power is of such importance as to merit experiment. I know a businessman whose imperturbability, inner peace and poise are impressive. Yet he confesses that his major problem was tension. But he discovered a workable technique for living without tension.

"I need to be renewed at least two times a day," he explained. "I retire into my private office at eleven o'clock each morning just when one begins to have a let-down feeling and spend two minutes in meditation. Again at four o'clock the time of the late-afternoon energy lag, I repeat the same process."

This two-minute period of meditation does not take the usual form of prayer. This man does not consider his problems during this period, but instead "thinks" about God. He dwells upon thoughts of God's peace. He affirms God's presence. He conceives of spiritual strength as flowing into his being. He reports that these four minutes per day result in so marked a refreshment that it amounts to a complete renewal of energy in body and fresh clarity of mind. He declares this daily practice to be far superior to "pick-me-ups" previously relied upon.

A young officer had been shot down on his thirty-first bombing mission. His plane cracked up, and so did he—not physically, but emotionally. The crash, plus the strain and tension of his job, put him into a serious nervous state.

"It's how I feel inside that makes it so hard," he explained. "I'd almost rather have lost a limb than to feel all the time like a volcano about to blow up. I feel as if I would burst into a hundred pieces, and there are times when I want to scream—to shriek. The worst of it is I can't sleep, and when morning comes I think, 'How will I ever get through this day?' I'm certainly shot." He concluded with this pathetic statement, "I'm sick of myself. I don't like living with myself any more."

No one could blame the poor fellow. He was drawn taut, like a stretched rubber band. He could not relax, or rest. There was no peace in him. Little wonder he felt about himself as he did.

I assured him that he could work out of this condition. I happened to know of some medicine that could help him, and told him about it.

"Do you pray?" I asked.

"I try to, but it's hard thinking of the words. My mind wanders and I get nervous," he replied, "so usually I end up by not praying very much." When asked if he tried to read the Bible, he stated that any kind of reading was impossible; he could not concentrate. It "got him all tensed up," he said; made him want to shriek.

This boy was in a bad state of nerves. However, his trouble was not in his body, but in his mind. Nervous states, tension, inner turmoil, are usually not caused by any physical damage, but rather by disorganization of thoughts. Of course, I realized it would be of little value to say, "Cheer up—you'll be all right. Have faith and pray." He needed to know "how" to do that.

I gave him the following advice: "When you go to bed tonight, practice relaxing. Raise your arms and let them fall limply by your sides. Repeat this three or four times. Think of your entire body as being filled with peace. Close your eyes lightly and think of the tension as going out of the eyelids. Try relaxing the eyelids by thinking of them falling shut limply, somewhat as your arms fell by your sides.

"Then lying relaxed with lights out, say, preferably out loud, or quietly under your breath if with others, the simple words, "The Lord is my Shepherd."

"Conceive of these words," I urged, "as a medicine which permeates your mind, sinking into the subconscious as you sleep; conceive that this medicine is extending its healing benefit through the entire body and deep into the soul." I suggested also that he repeat this process before arising in the morning.

The young officer tried this prescription; he really worked it, and it did him a vast amount of good. The old peace has now returned, the strain is gone. Remember—the trouble very likely is in your thought. Thoughts may be healed the same as a cut finger, only the medicine isn't iodine and salve; it's a much more effective healing agent—it is the thought of God's peace, His presence and power. It takes a thought to heal thoughts.

Sometimes our personal attitudes cause inner tension. A man told me that he would willingly trade his annual two-weeks vacation from his job for a two-weeks vacation from himself. Unfortunately that cannot be. We have to live with ourselves whether we like it or not, so the best course is to get so we can like it.

A friend of mine used to have a terrible time with himself. Everybody irritated him. He came into New York on a commuters' train each morning, and the people on the train got on his nerves. Much of the news he read in the paper made him mad. He was filled with resentments, not merely against people he knew, but also against people he saw, and people about whom he read and never saw. He ate his breakfast in a busy and crowded restaurant in the city, and the people there got on his nerves. "What's the matter with people nowadays?" he complained.

He finally discovered that it wasn't the people at all; that it was himself who was causing the irritation and tension. He really did not hate other people basically; he hated himself. He was a sensitive and sore personality, a bundle of antagonisms organized around one central antagonism, namely, his own dissatisfaction with himself. Of course, he derived no pleasure from living with himself. He was a personal civil war.

There are many people like this, poor souls; but there is an answer to this unhappy condition. This man found it. He could not change himself. There is not much point in trying that. So he asked God to change him. He then began practicing Christ's attitude toward people. Presently he found that people and things didn't irritate him any more. He found himself actually beginning to like people. People seemed different, but actually *he* was the one who was different. Naturally when one has good will be exudes it unconsciously, and this in turn brings out good will in others. At any rate life became different because he was different. Now he enjoys life because he enjoys himself. He eliminated the irritable drive of tension.

The foregoing experiences suggest the importance of definite exercises in reducing tension. The habitual practice of tested methods gets results. Some prescriptions for the healing of tension are medical, others psychological, others spiritual; and still others, perhaps, partake of all three.

Following is a simple "prescription" which I, and hundreds who have tried it, have found to be very effective.

Some years ago I was heavily borne down by the pressure of work, and fell into that frantic attitude of mind common to those who try to do too much in too short a time, or who at least have the notion that they are so doing, which is just as bad. The result was that I lost the capacity for sound, restful sleep. After tossing for several hours, I arose about three o'clock one morning in an acute state of tension. Instead of reclining in a relaxed attitude, I had been lying in bed doubled up, as if expecting that at any moment the bed would collapse and precipitate me onto the floor. My mouth was dry; I was restless and hot. I went into the library. I picked up several books, but none of them interested me. What book is interesting under such circumstances? I stomped restlessly about, finally stopping at the window which I opened. I put my head out and looked up and down Fifth Avenue.

It was raining, and the rain fell upon my head. I turned my face up to the rain, which fell cool and refreshing upon my face. It ran down until presently I could taste it and smell it. It occurred to me then that among all the things of this world which change, one thing never changes, and that is the taste and smell of rain. Even falling through the murky skies of Manhattan, it tasted and smelled just as it did years ago in Ohio; I remembered the old rain barrel at the corner of my boyhood home on a rainy day in May, when great pools where one splashed with bare feet formed under the trees. It gave a momentary sense of peace and refreshment to reflect upon the changelessness of the rain.

Finally I sat down in an easy chair and picked up a little

pamphlet. Leafing carelessly through it, I read:

"You are restless, you are tense. You are anxious and nervous. You cannot sleep."

"How in the world did you know that?" I cried in astonishment.

I continued reading. The writer said, "Practice a simple method of overcoming tension."

The pamphlet, which has long since disappeared (it contained little of value except the germ of an idea), suggested physical, mental and spiritual exercise which proved valuable. It being early in the morning, and having nothing else to do, I decided to try the suggestion offered. The method, later developed by additional experimentation, follows:

First of all, relax the body. To do this allow your head to fall back against the head rest of your chair. Let it drop back easily, not in any sense rigid, but as though the head were falling off your shoulders. Then stretch out your feet as far as possible, and push your toes beyond that, as far as you can extend them. Raise the arms and let them fall limply and naturally by the side. Allow your hand to fall upon your knee, like a wet leaf on a log. What is more relaxed than a wet leaf on a log!

Sit loosely in the chair with every muscle relaxed, allowing the chair to bear the full weight of the body so that if the chair were removed the body would fall inertly to the floor.

After the body has been relaxed, relax the mind. We have a marvelous gift which we call imagination. By imagination one may transport himself hundreds of miles over mountain and sea, and return in the fraction of an instant. it is the true magic carpet. By it you can take a vacation trip without paying for a ticket or moving from your own home.

Imagine that you are, for example, in the north woods, peacefully sitting with your back to a tree. The atmosphere is redolent of pine and cedar and hemlock. All is quiet, save the natural sounds of the forest. Before you is a lake, its blue waters unruffled, except for the occasional leap of a fish. Looking through the trees you can see in the far distance great mountains, lost in a mystic haze of blue, shoudering out the sky. The sunlight is falling mellow and warm upon the earth, splashing down through the trees and dancing on the water of the lake.

Following this method of relaxation, I found I was attaining not only a sense of rest in body, but also a pervading calmness of mind. The mind was being relaxed by taking it away momentarily from the problems agitating it and rendering it incapable of rational functioning and collected thought. This had been accomplished in just a flashing moment of time.

A quick turning of the mind in prayer while engaged in the busy activities of the day is like that. You do not need to go apart and kneel down to pray, although the posture of humility is helpful. Simply turn your thoughts to God. In so doing you are opening your mind to Him. He will do the rest.

The third and final element in this process of relaxation is the relaxation of the soul. The method is simple. Relax the soul by the exercise of spiritual thinking. Fix the mind on God. Think of God in whatever terms He is most understandable to you. People have many differing conceptions of God. When the name of God is spoken different minds instantly form varying pictures. But think of God in terms of His kindliness, His watchful care, His compassion and understanding.

In relaxing the soul, say to yourself words from the Scriptures which express peace and God's care. Among them use this verse from Isaiah: "Thou wilt keep him in perfect peace, whose mind is stayed on Thee."

Most people suffer tension because they keep their minds stayed or fixed, not on God, but at the far lower level of their personal troubles and anxieties.

Repeat quietly to yourself other healing passages: "Peace I give unto you: not as the world giveth, give I unto you. Let not your heart be troubled, neither let it be afraid." And again, "Come unto me, all ye that labor and are heavy laden, and I will give you rest."

The words of old hymns are often helpful such as the line from "Lead, Kindly Light"—"So long Thy power hath kept me, sure it *still* will led me on."

God has watched over you in the past. He can be depended upon to do so now and in the future.

As a result of this experience I quickly felt the desire for sleep. I was rested in body. Muscle and nerve relaxed. I was conscious of worries being lifted from the mind, and tension passing. There was a sense of peace deep within.

This process is not intended merely to induce sleep, but is a formula which may be employed in the busiest part of the most active day. Nor is it escape from active responsibility. It increases the capacity for active work. Power is derived from quietness.

Edwin Markham has a wise line: "At the heart of the cyclone tearing the sky is a place of central calm." The cyclone derives its power from a calm center. So does a man. Out of relaxation comes driving energy. Power is generated in and derived from a calm center.

Practice will reduce the time needed for this exercise, until it will require only a moment. By such technique, modified or expanded to suit your own personality, you may find complete relaxation and learn to live without tension.

Chapter Five

HOW TO THINK YOUR WAY TO SUCCESS

"Where do you get your successful ideas?" I asked a famous businessman. We were in his library.

"Upstairs in a little room," he answered. "Would you like to see it?"

He led me to a small room furnished with only a table and two chairs. Simple yet exquisite drapes hung at the windows. On opposite walls were two picture. One showed the Matterhorn capped with snow; the other pictured a swiftly flowing, sun-speckled trout stream, rushing over smooth stones and into deep pools. "Both pictures," he said, "represent peace. One portrays peace immovable, the other peace movable. Both aspects are necessary to the proper contemplation of peace," he remarked.

On the table was a pad, several pencils and a Bible.

"Here is where I get my ideas," he said.

He explained that his method is to come home from his office well in advance of the dinner hour and shut himself in this little room. There his privacy is never disturbed. He seats himself in an easy chair and consciously and deliberately relaxes his body. He does this by placing his feet firmly on the floor, raising his hands and letting them fall limply two or three times, saying as he does so, "My arms are dead, my arms are dead." He does the same with his feet, lifting them up and letting them drop. He also relaxes his eyelids by allowing them to fall a half dozen times as inertly as possible. This technique, he said, is quite effective in eliminating strain.

Next he reads from the Bible, selecting passages dealing with quietness, serenity, peace of mind. He knows where to find these quickly and I noticed that they were underscored. His favorite quotation is, "Let this mind be in you, which was also in Christ Jesus." (Philippians 2:5.)

"It is possible," he asserted, "to experience the quality of mind Christ had and to possess to a degree His insights and clarity of understanding."

The next procedure is to write down the particular problem upon which he wanted insight. It may be a business problem, or some personal matter, or a domestic quandary. Every factor pertaining to the problem is put down on paper. "Writing down an idea tends to clarity it," he declared. He quoted Themistocles, "Speech is like the cloth of Arras opened and spread abroad; whereas in thought it lies as in packs." When he has put down on paper everything he can think of in connection with the problem, he then studies and considers it, weighing and analyzing it.

The final procedure takes the form of a prayer somewhat as follows: "God, I feel relaxed in body and in mind. My little mind is not big enough to understand the intricacies and ramifications of my problems. I have tried to study this problem. I now ask you, God, to give illumination, insight, and understanding that I may take the proper course."

Having done this, he said, "I leave the room and put the problem out of my mind. I then spend the evening reading or conversing with friends. The answer may come in the midst of a conversation or I may be awakened in the night with the answer clearly in mind. Sometimes I may have to repeat this process several times, but," and he emphasized this with great earnestness, "whenever I have practiced this method of thinking, the right answers to my problems always come. The answer has not always been what I expected or wanted, but the answer I have received has been the right one when judged by the ultimate results."

This man had discovered that the ultimate in the art of thinking is the spiritual touch. He had learned how to think creatively. His emotional, spiritual and intellectual energies joined to deliver ideas that were sound and practical.

We need to cultivate practical techniques of thinking, for the power to think is one of our greatest faculties. Your life, or mine, is not determined by outward circumstances, but by the thoughts that habitually engage the mind. You create your own world by your thoughts. It has been said, "A man is what he eats." A deeper truth is, a man is what he thinks. The wisest of all books says, "As he thinketh in his heart, so is he." As a man thinks habitually in his conscious and sub-conscious mind, that is what he becomes.

Marcus Aurelius, wisest man of Rome, said, "Our life is what our thoughts make of it." Ralph Waldo Emerson, wisest American, said, "A man is what he thinks about all day long." Obviously a person thinks about many things in the course of a day. Beneath all of these thoughts, however, is one basic or primary thought. Into this fundamental thought, all other thoughts are drained, and from it, take their color and content.

For example, some people allow fear to become their primary thought. Fear usually begins as a thin trickle of worry across the mind. Repeated over many days, it becomes habitual until it cuts a deep channel across the consciousness. Every thought a man, to whom this has happened, thinks—about his family, about his business, about his health, or about the world—is colored by the basic and primary thought of fear and comes up tinctured with anxiety and insecurity. No matter how he resists the persistent thought of fear, he cannot escape it. He is what he thinks about all day long; he is a man of fear.

To counteract this condition—substitute a different and stronger basic thought. The only primary thought that can successfully oppose fear is faith or the positive thought. Only faith is stronger than fear.

But what is the technique for developing faith? It is to affirm the positive thought. Faith, too, begins as a thin trickle across the mind. Repeated, it becomes habitual. It cuts deeply into the consciousness until finally (to use a crude figure) you have two basic channels of thought—one of fear, and one of faith. But fear can never defeat faith. As you deepen the channel of the faith thought, the channel of the fear thought finally dries up. The faith thought overflows and becomes the deep, flowing, primary thought of the mind. Then every business, about your family, about the world is touched by the thought of faith and comes up bright, resplendent, optimistic and positive.

As a result of your new and positive caste of thought, you will learn to believe in yourself, in your country, and in the future of mankind. You will now have a deep, positive conviction that life is good. Shadows which once frightened you and obstacles which once defeated you flee away and are overcome. Physically you may be the same person, but mentally you are living in a different world. Actually you are a different person because you are thinking differently. You are what you think about all day long. But your thoughts now give you power and are leading you to happiness and success.

A thought, properly employed, possesses a healing property. Physicians today are emphasizing "psychosomatic" medicine; psycho—of the mind, and soma—of the body. They study the effect of thought or emotion upon physical states. For emphasis, a physician once said that he would have little trouble in getting most of his patients well if only he could cut off their heads during convalescence. And, in fact, chemical and organic conditions would frequently adjust themselves were it not for the effect of improper thinking. I would argue that every individual should have a regular check-up on his thought processes. A wise man has bodily check-ups to keep himself in physical health. Why not check-ups for mental health? The mind is surely as important, if not more so, than the body, for the body is largely regulated by the mind. Get your mind checked up.

The church may serve as a kind of re-conditioning center where a person can submit his mind for an overhauling and get it put back into order. Contrary to a popular misconception, psychiatry does not deal with pathological cases, but may be defined as a science which helps to keep normal people normal. The cure is often effected by the simple application of spiritual and psychiatric treatment.

A New York City businessman cam to our church clinic. He was a successful man holding a rather important position. By an extraordinary summoning of his energies, he was able to keep going. His expenditure of nervous energy was immense. He felt depleted in energy and had little strength and no zest. His mind was haunted by interlocking obsessions.

"What do I need?" he asked.

"Mental conditioning," I replied.

"What is mental conditioning?" he asked in some surprise.

"It is a process to freshen up the mind," I explained.

He told me that he was "no good until eleven o'clock in the morning." "I have an awfully hard time getting up, and when I do, I am disagreeable and unhappy until about eleven. Then I manage to perk up and do pretty well for a few hours."

"What time do you get up?" I asked.

"Around nine. I have a wonderful wife. She serves my breakfast in bed."

"Now isn't that sweet?" I said. "She comes in and says consolingly, 'How are you, sweetheart,' doesn't she?"

"Yes," he said, "how did you know?"

"And what do you do?" You groan, 'Oh, I feel so terrible!' Then she puts her soft hands lightly on your brow, and says, 'That's all right, sweetheart, you just lie there and I will bring you up some breakfast.' "

"Yes, that's what she does. Isn't that wonderful?"

"You haven't a wife. She is acting like a mother, babying you," I said.

"The doctor says there is nothing wrong with me except my mind," he continued. "He says I'm a victim of self-pity as a result of wrong-thinking."

"Your doctor is right," I said. "You need to have your mind re-conditioned. I suggest that you pray and ask for strength—then believe that strength is being given you. To-morrow morning when your wife comes into your room and asks how you are, give her a crisp, healthy answer. Say to her, 'I feel new strength—through God's help I know I'm all right.' Then get out of bed, and go singing in to shave."

"She would die of a heart attack," he said.

"Get downstairs," I continued, "and eat breakfast at the table. Get started to your office by nine o'clock." I thought it ought to be eight-thirty, but I didn't want to be too hard on him.

"That wears me out to think about it," he said.

"It's your thoughts that wear you out," I explained. "But you won't be tired if you conceive of God's energy as being yours."

I did not see him for quite a while. Then one day I met him on the street.

"Do you remember that mental conditioning business you told me about?" he asked. "Well, all the way down the street that day I thought, 'That man Peale is a fool. Mental conditioning—affirming I feel fine; of all the crack-brained notions.' Then I got to thinking maybe I really was not as bad off as I had been assuming. A few mornings later I was certain I felt better and decided to try out your suggestion. My wife came in and said, 'How are you?' 'Fine,' I answered, 'marvelous!' I leaped out of bed, swept her off her feet, kissed her and set her down hard, and went singing in to shave. You never saw such an expression on anybody's face. And—I had a good day and have been practicing your idea ever since. When a negative thought tries to sneak into my mind, I affirm that God is flooding my mind with peace and strength. I have found that when you affirm it, you have gone a long way toward having it."

People develop defeatist habits of thought which make them miserable. Their happiness is frustrated by their thinking. Things will be different when you think differently. When depressing thoughts come to mind, literally say, "You old, depressing defeat thought—get out of my mind. I can defeat you. I affirm that God's strength is in me." Actually talk back to your thoughts. At all cost conquer defeatist thinking, otherwise it will conquer you.

Get your mind renewed and life will be different!

An industrialist discovered the truth of this. He underwent a physical examination and the doctor said, "There is nothing wrong with you that cannot be cured by a new mental outlook on life." He charged plenty for this prescription and well he should, for it was sound advice. The industrialist went to his minister. He got his thinking changed—got the worry and fear thoughts out. Rid of the thoughts that were poisoning his mind, he is now a new man. He learned to think his way to success and happiness.

It is very important to keep the thought processes in good condition for in your mind are all of the paraphernalia needed to build your career. Keep your mind free from confusion and all the creative ideas you need will be yours. Your mind will deliver them to you if you keep your intellectual equipment well regulated.

An important factor in the achievement of success is the art of original and creative thinking. The average person does not trust his own mind to create for him the ideas which he needs. Business firms are beginning to realize the importance of creative thinking and in some instances have actually employed men for the sole purpose of thinking. They are not research men, but thinking men. Their job is to study the business, fill their minds full of it and then trust their minds to deliver fresh and creative ideas.

Dr. Glenn Clark quotes the late Arthur Brisband to the effect that there are many positions in this country which will pay a salary of fifty thousand dollars a year for thinking creative thoughts. These jobs go begging, he says.

It is said that John D. Rockefeller, Sr., once employed a man at twenty-five thousand dollars a year whose job was to sit in a swivel chair and think up new ideas for the business. A jealous person complained to Mr. Rockefeller, "Why do you pay that fellow twenty-five thousand dollars a year for swiveling around in a swivel chair and staring out the window?" Mr. Rockefeller said, "If you can think up as many good ideas as he does, I will give you twenty-five thousand dollars a year and a swivel chair." Do not conclude, however, from this incident that every man who swivels around in a swivel chair is worth twenty-five thousand dollars a year. Many are merely engaging in intellectual free wheeling.

May I at this point inject a homely parable? A man was hard pressed for money and he prayed and asked the Lord to give him some. The Lord, in His kindliness, heard the prayer coming up from earth and called one of his angels and said, "That poor fellow needs money. Send some down to him."

The angel returned and said, "Lord, I have looked through the vaults of heaven and can find no money. We have only that which 'neither moth nor rust doth corrupt, and where thieves do not break through nor steal,' but while we have no money, we have some wonderful ideas and insights. Shall we send some of those down to him?"

The man had continued to prayer and he showed great faith and the Lord was delighted and said, "Yes, open the windows of heaven and pour out so many insights and ideas that he will have more than he needs."

And so it happened that everybody said, "What a creative, ingenious, resourceful mind this man possesses." This parable is as sound as the good earth on which we walk.

If you do honest and thorough intellectual work, the next step is to relax your mind, trusting it to sort the material and deliver insights and solutions to problems. The best kind of thinking is that which is done unconsciously after conscientious study and preparation. Professor Brand Blanshard, professor of philosophy at Yale, and former President of the American Philosophical Association, tells us that great writers employed the art of unconscious thinking. He describes the method of several.

"Stevenson, when he had a story to write, would block out the plot and then leave the detail to his 'Brownies,' the little people who worked during sleep in the hidden places of his mind. Henry James has described how, in writing *The American*, he took his main idea and 'dropped it for the time into the deep well of unconscious cerebration,' where it went on to take form and substance. Milton, for long periods, would brood over a theme and write nothing. But during these 'droughts,' as he called them, the springs were forming beneath the surface and suddenly, in the middle of the night sometimes, he would call for his daughters to catch, from dictation, the torrent of verse that came welling up. People used to wonder at the pulpit fertility of Beecher; he once preached daily for eighteen months without missing a day; and his sermons were powerful ones. But he has left it on record that the work was largely unconscious. He kept a number of themes ripening at once in the cellars of his mind; a week or so before the sermon was due, he would select one that was well along, consider it a while intently, then commit it again to the cellar. On the morning of delivery he would find that it had germinated into a large mass of relevant ideas which he would then order and put down at tremendous speed.

"Nor is it only in art and letters that unconscious thinking has been used; it has solved some of the knottiest problems of the sciences.

"Thus Gauss had been working on a theorem in arithmetic for four years, after which 'as a sudden flash of light the enigma was solved.' But he explicitly adds that he was unable to see the thread he must have followed in reaching this end result.

"I have found," says Bertrand Russell, "that if I have to write upon some rather difficult topic, the best plan is to think about it with very great intensity—the greatest intensity of which I am capable—for a few hours or days, and at the end of that time give orders, so to speak, that the work is to proceed underground."*

Here is an example that could well be added to Professor Blanshard's list. Mr. Robert G. LeTourneau, famed industrialist and world's largest builder of earth-moving machinery, has the genius to invent very complicated machinery. On occasion during World War II, the government ordered certain types of machines, as, for example, one able to pick up broken planes. It was needed quickly. Mr. LeTourneau and his

---

*Brand Blanshard, *The American Mercury*, December, 1945, p. 693.

assistants went to work on it but were getting nowhere. The solution did not come.

It happened to be prayer meeting night and Mr. LeTourneau is never absent. He said to his assistants, "I am going to prayer meeting. Perhaps the solution will come while I am in the meeting." He put the problem entirely out of his conscious thought, went to the prayer meeting where he fully gave himself to the spirit of worship. Before the meeting was over, the entire machine was pictured in his mind. He had only to go back and set down the blueprint.

One of the outstanding practical thinkers in American business is Beardsley Ruml, often referred to as America's number one idea man.

"Ruml's method of tackling problems is to sit in a chair and do nothing. He has advised executives who have problems on their hands to lock themselves up, sit in a chair, and do nothing for at least an hour a day. It is essential for apprentices at musing, that there should be no newspapers or other reading matter around to break the spell. Ruml spends much more than an hour a day in sessions of this kind. With his mind released from ordinary influence, he can command wider vistas of fact and theory than when methodically studying a subject.

"He has described the mental condition in which he gets his ideas as 'a state of dispersed attention.'

"Although information helps, it is not necessary to know everything about a problem, according to Ruml, in order to tackle it in reverie, or waking-dream fashion. He thinks nothing of letting his subconscious mind wander through regions in which his knowledge is very rarefied. His farm plan is an example of an idea picked out of remote space; Ruml was profoundly ignorant of the farm problem at the time. He is highly educated and has investigated many subjects, but he is not a typical scholar. He reads comparatively little. His career tends to vindicate the old philosopher Hobbes, who said, 'If I read as much as other men, I would know as little as they do.'

"Ruml doesn't proceed from premise to conclusion or follow any known logical method in inventing his plans. He doesn't seem to hear voices or receive messages. His faculty is unusually described as clairvoyance or intuition, two unsatisfactory words which fail to throw much light on what actually goes on in his mind."*

In one industry a "silent room" has been set aside for executives where without books or other paraphernalia they may have solitude to practice the art of creative thinking.

Dr. Frederick Kettner, authority on youth training, considers the practice of creative silence a vital part of education. Silence brings about remarkable changes in young people. He makes the unique suggestion that the architecture in the modern age should include a "silence" room in each home where man can figuratively wash his brain and heart. Many modern homes include a "rumpus" room, primarily intended for the children. Judging from current domestic situations, it would seem that there are altogether too many "rumpus" rooms in homes. We need more "silence" rooms.

A successful sales manager says it isn't necessary to have a room in which you may go apart; one may practice the art of retirement into mental quietness even in the midst of confusion.

---

*Alva Johnston, *The New Yorker*, February 10, 1945.

His method is to remove his glasses and put his hands over his eyes for a half minute. In this half minute he deliberately thinks of a peaceful scene, such as the place he fished last summer, or a mountain view. Having allowed this picture to flash into his mind, he then says quietly to himself the following words, repeating the sentence several times, "Peace is flooding my mind, my body, and my soul." He declares that he feels peace flowing in upon him by the act of conceiving it as doing so. He turns to his work with the feeling that a refreshing of his thought processes has taken place. Dullness and haziness lift and energy and new perceptions are given him.

An outstanding investment banker in New York told me that he considers the reading of the Bible the most valuable method of clarifying and stimulating his mind. He goes to his office in the financial district at seven-thirty in the morning and spends the first half hour reading the Bible. He then has fifteen minutes of quiet meditation after which he says he is ready for the day's work. He is an accomplished linguist and some days reads the Bible in French, other times in Spanish, claiming that the differing emphases given by these languages, add to his insights.

Recently he went to another city on an important banking mission. For two hours of his journey he studied business reports affecting the negotiations. For the next hour, he said, "I read St. Paul—mark you, not merely for spiritual values, but primarily for the stimulation of my mental processes. Finally I had fifteen minutes of relaxing prayer and meditation, after which I went to sleep. Upon arrival at my destination I did not try to sell the people anything they did not want or need. I merely laid all the facts before them as I had thought them out. I then returned to New York. Two days later I had on my desk a large amount of business." Had no financial results materialized he would have been satisfied with the knowledge that he had done all within his power.

"You really think that this practice has clarified your thinking?" I asked.

"I do not think it, I *know* it," he answered firmly.

Chapter Six

PRAYER—THE MOST POWERFUL FORM OF ENERGY

Early one morning I arrived at the Grand Central Station in New York and took a taxi to my home. The driver proved to be a very happy and friendly man.

"You're up bright and early this morning," I commented.

"Oh!" he replied, "I am here every morning at this time; that is, every morning except Sunday."

"And what do you do on Sunday?" I asked.

"Why, what do you suppose?" he replied. "I go to church." He stopped for a traffic light. "That isn't the whole of it," he said. "I sing in the choir also. I like the old hymns, don't you?"

Upon my agreement, he suddenly offered, "Would you like me to sing a hymn for you?"

This was astonishing, but one learns to expect almost anything in New York, so I said, "Yes, I would like to hear you sing." At this he broke into one of the old hymns, which he sang in a clear tenor voice as we rolled down Fifth Avenue.

When he had finished I complimented him, and then asked, "Have you a good minister in your church?"

"A good minister!" he exclaimed. "We have the best in New York and I don't mean maybe!"

This pleased me, for I always like to meet a man who is

enthusiastic about his minister. Just then he went past my own church at the corner of Fifth Avenue and Twenty-ninth Street.

"There is where I go to church," I told him.

"Is that so?" he replied. "Do you have a good minister there?"

"Well," I said, "only so-so; you see, I happen to be the minister myself."

This unexpected information nearly caused him to run up on the sidewalk.

"I guess I took in too much territory back there," he said.

When we arrived at my home we chatted for a minute.

"I'll tell you why my minister means so much to me," he said. "I haven't always been a taxi driver. I had a good business once, but it went down in the depression, I knew that God had a plan for me, and He didn't fail me. My minister got me into the taxi business. He said, 'Bill, running a taxi is the same as operating any business. If you give good service, if you are friendly, if you treat people right and trust in God, you will get along, and you'll have a good time doing it.'

"My minister told me that every morning when I went over to the garage to get my cab, *before I started out*, I was to bow my head over the wheel and dedicate my day's work to God and to people. That may sound pious, but I want to tell you that I have made a good living. What's more, I have had a wonderful time, and I am very happy; happier than I have ever been before."

I say without qualification that here was a man who combined good business practices with his religion, and was a success in life. I haven't the slightest doubt that this man has by now gone on to greater things, because he has the philosophy that works: trust God, work hard, put your business in God's hands, and serve people.

This taxi driver utilized a procedure which one of the world's foremost scientists, Alexis Carrel, highly recommended. He said, "The most powerful form of energy one can generate is prayer, Prayer, like radium," he continued, "is a luminous and self-generating form of energy."

Alexis Carrel, whose political aberration does not vitiate his scientific knowledge, made that astounding statement to a generation that is perfectly familiar with power in its most dramatic forms. Yet, points out this scientist, the most powerful form of energy one can generate is not mechanical, electronic or even atomic energy, but prayer energy.

Most of us are novices in prayer. Many seldom pray, some do not pray at all. There are, generally speaking, three ways in which men get what they want and need: (1) by work, (2) by thought, (3) by prayer. The first two are used every day. The third is greatly neglected.

Why? Probably because work and thought are obvious factors of our everyday experience. They are common, everyday things, while prayer is associated with something different, with special forms and postures. It has been made a sort of Sunday-go-to-meeting thing remote from our daily lives.

This elimination of the prayer factor from man's experience is a tragic omission. It compels us to bear the entire weight and burden of life. Little wonder men break down, or fail to achieve the best possible. Through spiritual procedures we may make contact with a tremendous source of strength. Greater strength may be generated by prayer than by the thoughts of the brain or the working of the hands. Let me repeat: the most powerful form of energy one can generate is prayer energy.

The connection between men and the universe may be far more subtle and profound than we may think. We are part of nature and of God, and to truly succeed in life one must harmonize himself with nature and God.

A brilliant woman recovered from a long and serious illness and went to Florida to recuperate. She went to Daytona Beach, one of the most beautiful beaches in the world. During her convalescence it was her custom daily to lie on the beach to get the sun. No one was near her. Alone in the midst of mature, she practiced deliberately turning her mind toward God. She prayed deeply.

One day she became acutely conscious of the deep silence of nature. She felt strangely attuned to the world. The quietness was such that to her astonishment, she could actually hear her own heart beat. She began to count those beats. She noticed the rhythm, steady and undeviating. She was listening to the beating of her own heart as it sent the life-blood coursing through her body.

As she lay listening to her heart beat, she turned her eyes and looked through the beach grass near her, washed clean and fresh by the tides. Her eyes selected one particular blade of beach grass. She watched as it was moved slowly and gracefully to and fro by a gentle breeze. She was amazed to discover that it moved with virtually the same rhythm and beat as her heart.

Then her eyes lifted to the sea. Sprinkled with sunshine like myriads of diamonds, sparkling in the sunlight, it rolled majestically inward in long foamy curlers upon the clean sand. Her mind suddenly became alive to the amazing fact that the beating of the waves upon the beach was also in rhythm not dissimilar to the waving of the grass and the beating of her heart. She became aware of one fundamental rhythmic harmony. Then came a realization that she was at one with nature, that she was a constituent part of its inner harmony. This though caused all loneliness and fear to leave her mind. Now she knew that she was in tune with God, that God's healing forces were flowing through her bringing back bodily health. This brought a deep peace and feeling of renewal.

"I shall never be afraid of anything again," she declared "For now I know there is a power by which life can be recreated. I know the secret of attuning to that power." It is a medium through which the close connection of man to God is achieved.

To be efficient in prayer you must learn the art of praying. It is a mistake to think that the laws of efficiency do not apply to prayer. Obviously skills are required in the operation of all power. It is not reasonable to assume that no skill is required in the exercise of the greatest power of all. Yet in mastering the art of prayer it is only necessary to follow certain simple principles. You do not have to go to college or technical school to become an expert in this field.

The first step in learning to pray is just to pray. You can read every book ever written about prayer, and you can attend innumerable discussions on prayer, but still the only way to learn to pray is to pray.

As a young man I took lessons in public speaking. Some time later I met one of the greatest orators of that period and asked him, "How does one become proficient as a public speaker?"

"By speaking," he replied. "Learn the art by practice. Speak every time you get a chance. Keep doing it. Keep practicing constantly, seeking to improve yourself."

That advice applies to all efficiency. It is important to study the rules and techniques of anything you want to master, but in the last analysis you learn by doing.

How much time each day do you spend in prayer? I have asked that question of many people and have arrived at the conclusion that about five minutes per day is the probable average. Some pray more than that; some less—most people probably less.

Let us try a little arithmetic. The average person is awake about sixteen hours a day. That means he has 960 minutes at his disposal. If he uses only five minutes to pray, it means that he is praying only one half of one per cent of his waking hours. There was a time during prohibition days when according to an act of Congress one half of one per cent of alcohol in a beverage was legally declared to be non-intoxicating. This percentage is non-intoxicating in religion also. Raise the daily percentage of time you spend in prayer if you expect to experience its power.

Again I quote Alexis Carrel: "When we pray we link ourselves with the inexhaustible motive power that binds the universe. Pray everywhere; in the street, in the subway, in the office, the shop, the school, as well as in the solitude of one's own room or in a church. True prayer is a way of life. Today as never before prayer is a binding necessity in the lives of men and nations."

A practical plan is to practice utilizing spare moments that would otherwise be aimless. I know a young woman who lives in Brooklyn and works in Manhattan. She formerly spent the fifteen minutes required for the subway journey by just sitting and staring at the advertisements around the car. Then one day she hit upon the expedient of closing her eyes and reciting quietly to herself the Lord's prayer and a few verses of scripture. She would pray about her work for that day and also pray for various people. Having a rather witty way of expression, she told me that the distance between her home and her office was "three Lord's prayers and three Twenty-Third Psalms." Thus she gets in thirty minutes of prayer each day on the subway. Out of these thirty minutes during which she formerly reshuffled her worries, she now draws inspiration for a singularly happy and useful life.

My friend, Frank Lauback, a famous educator, utilizes time spent in a bus to pray for his fellow passengers. He fixes his eye on each one in turn and prays for him or her. People who know him have commented on the amazing manner in which this radiation of love and goodwill changes the atmosphere of a bus. Laubach picturesquely says he just sits in a bus and "swishes love all over the place." One day a sour-faced man sitting in front of him to whom he had said nothing suddenly turned around and growled, "What this country needs is a religious revival." Apparently this kind of praying is contagious. If you do no more than make some of your otherwise aimless minutes prayer minutes you will soon notice new strength and joy welling up within you.

Prayer responds to law as does any science. Learn these laws and practice them and you will inevitably get a definite result. One of the primary laws of prayer is simplicity. Make your prayers simple and natural. It is not necessary to use stereotyped phrases and words. Talk to God as to a friend.

I learned a great deal about prayer from my grandmother.

She lived in a little town in the Midwest, in an old-fashioned house, typical of that region. There was a romance about the old-fashioned house. My grandmother's heating plant was a wood-burning stove. One side of you was warm and the other side freezing. Never in her lifetime did she have modern refrigeration. Her butter and eggs were placed in a crock outside the door. She was a strong, simple, old-fashioned woman.

My brother and I used to spend our summers with her. She took us over from our parents. After supper (dinner was the noon-day meal in those days) she would read to us by a kerosene lamp. Her concave lenses sat rather far down on her nose as she read stories to us.

Then she would take us upstairs to bed. It was a great high-posted bed laid with handmade quilts, and had an old-fashioned featherbed mattress in which we would sink so far that only our ears protruded. She would put the lamp on a stand and kneel by our bed. On her knees she would talk to the Lord, as to one with whom she was well acquainted and—as I see it now—to reassure us.

"O Lord," so her prayer ran, "I hate to put these two little fellows away off here in this bedroom. When I take this light away it is going to be very dark, and they are so little. They may be scared, but they do not need to be, because You are here, and You are going to watch over them all through the night. You will watch over them all their life long too, if they are good boys. Now, Lord, I ask You to watch over the pillows of these little fellows this night."

Then she would take the lamp, the glow fading upon the wall as she passed from the room. Her soft footfalls died away as she passed down the steps. On stormy nights, especially when the wind would howl around the house, my brother and I would huddle together in that big bed. I used to look up in the darkness and in imagination see a great, kindly face looking down on my pillow. I have always thought there was something magnificent about that prayer, "Look down upon the pillow of these little fellows."

My grandmother said, "Remember, God is not some Oriental potentate sitting upon a throne; He is your friend; He is right by your side. Talk to Him in simple, plain language, telling Him what is on your heart, and He will listen to you."

Make your prayers simple. If you are sitting at your desk and you do not know what to do about some matter, do not call your partner, because he may not know, either; but call in a greater Partner. Merely say, "Lord, I am stuck with this business problem. You know more about this business than I do; tell me what to do." If your fears and anxieties are heavy, talk to God about them in simple fashion. Then do your best and leave the rest to Him. Quit worrying about the things. God's love will protect and defend you. Trust Him, work hard, think straight, and things will come right.

In learning this art we need to recognize that prayer is a very simple thing. We have, perhaps, made it too stilted and formal. A professor under whom I studied was one of the most God-like men I ever knew. I learned much about prayer from him. I liked to hear him pray in college chapel. When he prayed I surreptitiously watched him. His lifted face lighted up—an outward reflection of an inner light. His hair, what there was of it, was snowy white. To his students, he was a human and practical saint whom we loved. Though now he is gone, we who studied under him shall never forget him. His name was Reverend Doctor George H. Butters,

D.D., Ph.D., LL.D., but to his students he was "Daddy" Butters. Even in the classroom we sometimes called him "Daddy," but he never minded that.

He used to tell us that he had a difficult time with his wife in the matter of prayers. It seems that his wife was what he called a "rigid Christian," who believed that the only way to say one's prayers at night was to kneel down by the bedside. Sometimes it got very cold in the New England town where he lived, and his wife was a fresh air enthusiast! When bedtime came, the wind would be whistling through the room, impelling one to get ready for bed in a hurry. Mrs. Butters throve on the cold, and when she discovered that her husband had crept into bed, she would quietly, but firmly ask, "George, have you said your prayers?"

"No, my dear," would come the meek reply. "I am saying them in bed."

"George, you get out of bed and say your prayers in a proper manner."

Obediently but painfully he would slip out of bed, down to the cold floor, the cold wind whipping across his bare feet.

"On those occasions," he commented, "my prayers were short and to the point."

I remember his telling this in one of the most dignified churches in the city of Boston, to the delight of a distinguished congregation; real people always like a human being for a preacher. To "Daddy" Butters God was a friend. God was with him when he sat down to lunch. He was with him at his desk, in his office, when he rode on the train—He was with him everywhere. He talked about God as we would talk about a good friend. His entire cast of mind was that of one who lived with God. Life to him was itself a prayer. But he was never a kill-joy. I think of him as one of the happiest, most genuine, down-to-earth human beings I ever knew.

People who have this simple contact with God, have power. No matter how much difficulty, hardship, pain, tragedy and futility may come to them, they rise above it magnificently.

It cannot be over-emphasized that an important technique of prayer is to do all you can, then leave it to God. Put your hand to your problem with force and vigor, fully utilizing your own brain and effort; then put it into God's hands through prayer. A prominent New York physician recently told me that while this idea sounds simple, it contains a very profound and vital truth. He found this out from a critical experience, for he was taken ill and had to undergo a very serious operation. As a physician, he knew that the mortality rate for this particular operation was alarmingly high, that the chances for coming through were slight indeed. Naturally this realization caused him to be very greatly disquieted. His professional career was at the peak. He wanted to live.

He decided to practice prayer. He had secured the best scientific earthly help obtainable. Having done all that he could possibly do, he then simply put the matter in God's hands. He calmly rested himself upon God's will and wisdom. He told the Lord he did not want to die, that he wanted to live. He told the Lord that he had the best doctors available; that now having done all that any human being could do he was willing to leave the outcome to Him. However God wanted it to be, he as willing to accept.

He reports that immediately a sense of peace came into his mind and with it confidence. He said he felt inwardly that it would be all right however it turned out. He went into the operation with every human and divine force, free and unimpeded. He regained his health, and today is back at work every day performing one of the most difficult and skillful operations known to the medical profession.

A businessman in New York learned by practice the value of prayer in his business activity. "In the morning," he says, "I am usually the first to reach my office. I ask God to guide my efforts during the day, and I thank Him in advance for answers to my prayer. Before starting out to interview prospective customers it is my practice to pray by name for each man. I do not pray that I may make a sale, for emphasis upon self-interest tends to break the circuit. It would be dictating to God who may not want a sale made on that particular visit, or on any other visit for that matter. I merely pray for my customer as a person and ask that God may bless him in all his problems.

"The result," he continued, "is that I meet my customers in an atmosphere of friendliness and confidence. I have often noted that we are strangely attuned. Moreover, I have been privileged to help people whom otherwise I would never have contacted. This procedure lifts business above money-making to the plane of human understanding. Of course, it results ultimately in material blessings, not through any mysterious process but simply by being right with God and man. I am able to keep calm and handle each problem as it arises, and in strange ways overcome difficulties which in former years would have floored me completely." Let us turn from this successful businessman to a San Francisco woman who was in despair.

By accident this woman heard a radio talk by the author—a talk dealing with the simple and practical techniques of prayer. She wrote as follows:

This is my story—as briefly as I can put it—a big story to put in a few words.

In the summer of 1943, one afternoon I turned on the radio—something I seldom if ever do during the day. My next impulse was to turn it off when a sentence caught my ear. I waited for the next sentence and so on till I found myself sitting down by the radio and listening.

I always called myself a Christian, prayed, etc. but for the first time in my life something happened. That afternoon I first heard you, I was in the depths of despair. Things were going from bad to worse until it seemed involuntary bankruptcy was confronting me. Real estate salesmen seemed powerless. From that very afternoon I got a new grip—a new way of praying, I guess. I feel I was led, literally led, step by step to the office door of a woman broker across the Bay, whom I had never even heard of before. She took hold of the properties with vigor, even developed new qualities in them. It would take pages and pages to give you the story.

But, and here is the next great step. I have always had a desire to make designs. I talked very hard to God—asked him to show me definitely what to do. I received word that a two-yard drapery length of mine which I had sent to an International Textile Exhibition had received the first award. This has led to wonderful contacts with some of the best and most reliable firms. They wanted my designs. I am relating all this modestly, with reserve and deep sincere thanks to Our Lord and Father. It is a sample of the way the impossible becomes possible when God is the partner.

People who practice the simple techniques of prayer secure guidance to an unusual degree. They are directed in their activities and contacts by an invisible but definite power. In meeting situations and in dealing with people, they acquire remarkable skill. I do not, of course, believe that there is anything magical in prayer, but from my experience I do feel certain that insights, leads, and illuminations are given to people who habitually practice an attitude of prayer, in which they become amenable to divine guidance. I have seen enough indications of the validity of this statement that I accept it as a scientific injunction, to wit: Yield your mind with its problems to an attitude of prayer. Be willing to accept not what you want or what you think ought to be, but affirm that you will be led in the solution of your problem. The result will be that over a period of time you will clearly see the outlines of a pattern which you, yourself, did not conceive.

John G. Ramsay, Public Relations Representative of the United Steel Workers of America (C.I.O.), told me about a mutual acquaintance who spends one hour each day in prayer. Ramsay smiled and said, "I could not do that. I get enough suggestions from God in two minutes to keep me busy all day long." John Ramsay says that he gets guidance and direction for his daily work from these two minutes of prayer. Here is an example he relates.

"Some months ago I sat down at a table for four in a dining car. Three other men were already seated; as I later discovered, none was acquainted with the other. They all seemed gloomy and depressed. As I do not like to eat a meal in such an atmosphere, I began a conversation which I hoped would lift their spirits. Soon we were talking animatedly—mostly about religion.

"After we finished dinner, one said to me, 'I'd like to talk with you for a few minutes.'

" 'Certainly,' I replied, 'let's go into the lounge car.'

"The Lord must have wanted this conversation to be held, for even though the train was crowded two seats, side by side, awaited us. My new companion told me that when he left home as a boy, his father enjoined him never to allow more than ten minutes to elapse upon a train before talking to the nearest person about his religious life.

" 'On my first train ride,' he said, 'I was seated next to a burly fellow, I kept my eye upon my watch until ten minutes had passed; then, scared to death, I blurted out, 'Are you saved?' I got the rough answer you might expect, and for twenty years I have never spoken to another man about religion.

" 'Today,' he continued, 'you got three men, none of whom had met the other, to talking about religion naturally and interestingly in a couple of minutes. What's your technique?'

"We chatted for some time and, as he rose to leave, he introduced himself as vice president of a certain steel company; then he asked me my name and business.

" 'I am John Ramsay,' I replied. 'I am organizer for the United Steel Workers of America, and it is my job to organize the employees of your company.'

"Despite differences in point of view, we established fellowship and understanding based upon our common religious faith. I have never thought much about my 'technique,' except that it is to try to live a God-centered life."

This book emphasizes scientific spiritual principles which have been demonstrated in the laboratory of personal experience. Principles of guidance, of prayer, of faith, of simple trust, of relaxation, are presented not as theory, but as the Q.E.D. of actual test. Everything in this book is factual.

Whatever your problem, no matter how difficult, you can release spiritual power sufficient to solve your problem. The secret is—*pray* and *believe*. Even though it may be hard to believe, do it nevertheless. Simply believe that Almighty God will give His power to you. Pray and mentally yield yourself to God's power. Do this by affirming that you have not sufficient power within yourself and that, therefore, you are willing to put yourself completely in contact with spiritual force. The basic secret of the Christian religion is not effort or will power, important as they are. The secret of Christianity is faith. The only struggle it urges you to exert is the effort to believe. The art is to learn to have faith. When you have done so you become a channel through which divine power flows. It flows through *you*. You then have all the strength you need to meet any situation involving you.

An an illustration, here is the personal experience of a man who was "through." From brilliant success he plunged downward; then, at an age when many men retire, he came back. Here is a story that will thrill many—told in the man's own words.

"For upwards of fifty years my life was like a song. Then, for four years I never smiled. I had a lovely wife, three fine sons and a beautiful home. In business, mine was what people call a success story. At forty-seven, I was a Lieutenant Colonel in World War I, in charge of millions of dollars of supplies. At fifty, I was president of a large oil company. At fifty-eight, I was a close associate of one of Wall Street's leading figures. I was on top. Life was good, and I believed that although trouble might come to others, it would not come to me—well, just because it couldn't.

"Suddenly, all went wrong. I was one of the spectacular wrecks of the depression. I lost everything—my personal fortune, the home I loved, quickly, followed by the death of my wife, my idyllic companion for thirty-three years. To climax all my troubles, I was taken with encephalitis, a form of the dread sleeping sickness.

"After many weeks, I was pronounced cured, but there were scars in my emotional system.

"I was looked over by some of the best men in the medical profession, who said, 'Nothing is wrong with you.' I knew there was but, as I look back now, I see that my trouble was not in their line. So I went from neurologist to neurologist, from osteopath to osteopath, from diet faddist to diet faddist. Steadily I lost weight, gained in irritability and became more and more of a trial to my family and friends.

"When I returned to business I got no better; I became a neurasthenic and a hypochrondriac of the worst sort. Nothing that anyone said to me that could have been helpful, made the slightest impression. I thought constantly of my troubles, which I sought to unload upon other people. In street-cars I would my woes to anyone who would listen—friend or stranger.

" 'John,' said a friend to me, after I found a new life, 'do you remember an afternoon when I rode uptown with you on the subway? You talked all the way about your illness and your troubles. Finally, I told you I had an engagement, and left the train at Fourteenth Street, just to get away from you.'

"I know now, but didn't then, what a pest I was. The way I carried on, I was the only man in the world who had any troubles. I was resentful and venomous, and I cursed everything in general. Each morning, upon waking I asked myself, 'How in the name of God can I go through with another day?' I found myself hoping that some morning I wouldn't wake up. One day I sat in a hotel lobby, a farewell letter in my hand, deliberating from ten in the morning until late afternoon whether to leap from a top-floor window. I know now that my real trouble was not with my body but with my spirit.

"During this time I made two half-hearted ventures into realms of thought control and of religion. They had helped others, but my faith was weak. My attitude was: 'Well, God, I don't believe You can do anything about this situation, but let's see You try!'

"And to myself I said, 'This requires a miracle, and the days of miracles are past.' Nothing came of these ventures, of course, because there was no faith. But four years after I was stricken, the light of health and happiness dawned upon me in such a way that it could have been only God-directed.

"I was walking down a narrow street, carrying a cane which I used to think I needed, when I inadvertently struck a man who was passing me. Turning to apologize, I found him to be a genial person with an office in the same building with me. He asked me to call, which I did. I found him to be an ardent believer in the power of religious faith. He urged me to put my life in God's hands, to surrender all my troubles to Him and to practice thinking about God instead of myself.

"I was taught to pray and to have faith. This was the turning point in my life.

"It was pointed out to me that my thinking was all wrong; that the first thing I had to do was clear out my mind. (As a man thinketh, so is he.) This is the stuff I cleaned out of my mind! Self-pity, ill-will, fears and other evils. No wonder I was sick. This was the first real mental catharsis I had ever known and it was effective because it was done on a spiritual basis, under the direction of an understanding man.

"After this mental cleansing my friend began to feed my mind on simple, spiritual, wholesome food. I was given a course of reading lessons in spiritual truth. I was shown how to read the Bible. I discovered that the main part of the know-how is just to read it. I purchased one of those Bibles in which the words of Jesus are marked and also I read the Psalms. After reading I would sit quietly, with the thought that these words were passing through my mind like medicine.

"This person also taught me how to use my mind positively rather than negatively. Instead of dwelling mentally upon my troubles, I learned to affirm, in my own mind, that God was helping me at that very minute. Gradually this idea took possession of me. I found that one does become what he affirms he is when he does it in God's name.

"I practiced living with Christ in my mind, often talking to Him as though He were right with me (I know He is). My mind was flooded with a healing sense of peace. I felt myself becoming a new man, fulfilling one of the greatest and truest of all Bible texts: 'If any man be in Christ, he is a new creature: old things are passed away; behold, all things are become new.'

"This new-found power changed everything. I recovered gradually the zest I once had for work. A friend said to me.

'You are yourself again; it's a miracle!'

"Only God could have done this to me and shown the inner reservoirs of peace and strength which are in me now. Within a year God had helped me to become one of the big producers of my company. In succeeding years I have done an annual business of more than one-half million dollars. I claim no credit for this—merely mention it to show what God can do. This may sound materialistic, but it isn't. I cite it only to show the return of strength and power inwardly.

"Some months ago I met the head doctor of one of the big psychiatric clinics I once attended. He asked me how I was. 'Fine,' I replied. 'I've found something which really helped me.' Then I told him of my recovery. 'Well,' he observed, 'we work along the same line, except for excluding the religious element.'

" 'Yes,' I told him, 'that's what's the trouble with it.' Although the clinic was the last word in psychiatry, it was not until I found 'the religious element' that anything happened to me."

The man of this story discovered and put into practice the laws governing prayer and as a result was remade.

Now to sum up. Learn to pray correctly, scientifically. Employ tested and proved methods. Avoid slipshod praying. To guard against perfunctory praying, here are ten rules for saying your prayers. They have proved to be an effective, workable discipline of prayer.

1. Set aside a few minutes to be alone and quiet. Relax body, mind and spirit by turning the thoughts away from problems and fixing the mind on God. Think about Him in the way that is most natural.

2. Talk to God simply and naturally, telling Him anything that is on your mind. Do not think you have to use formal words and phrases. Talk to Him in your own language. He understands it.

3. Practice talking to God as you go about the business of the day. On the subway or bus, or at your desk, close your eyes for a moment to shut out the world and have a word or two with God. This will remind you of his presence and give you a sense of His nearness.

4. Affirm the fact that God is with you and helping you. That is to say, do not always beseech God for His blessings, but affirm the fact that He is now giving you His blessings.

5. Pray with the thought that your prayers reach out and surround your loved ones with God's love and care.

6. Think positive, not negative, thoughts when you pray.

7. Always state in your prayer that you are willing to accept God's will, whatever it is. Ask him for what you want, but express your willingness to take what He wants.

8. In your prayer simply put everything into God's hands. Pray for strength to do your best, and with confidence leave the rest to God.

9. Say a word of prayer for people who do not like you or have treated you badly. This will help them and release tremendous power in you.

10. At some time during every day say a word of prayer for this troubled world, for our country and for a lasting peace.

Then—*believe* that your prayers will be answered. "What things soever ye desire, when ye pray, *believe* that ye receive them, and ye shall have them."

Chapter Seven

FORGET FAILURES AND GO AHEAD

One of the most important of all skills is that of forgetting. It is said that a man is what he thinks, or what he eats. A man is also what he forgets.

I am not straining to be paradoxical when I say that to be happy and successful you must cultivate the ability to say to yourself—forget it! It may not be easy, neither is it as hard as you think, but—one thing is certain, you must learn to forget.

Memory is one of the greatest of our faculties. The ability to retain information and experience is of vital importance. But it is a more subtle art to be able to cast out of the mind—or at least from a commanding place in it—failures, events, unhappy things that should be forgotten. It is a great skill to be able to be selective and say, "I will hold this in cherished memory. This other I shall cast from me." To be efficient, to be happy, to have full control of your powers, and to go ahead successfully, you must learn how to forget.

Anyone who deals with personality problems in an intimate way is bound soon to become aware of the importance of forgetting. In dealing with people one finds that their problems really center around a few simple propositions—fear, guilt, selfishness, self-centeredness, and the inability to forget.

I know a top executive, who has risen by hard effort and marked ability to an important position, but he will not hold it unless he learns to forget. He is a man of considerable rigidity and wants everything to be just so. His wife died recently. He thinks of her as the finest person he ever knew. But she was rather carefree, while he was rigid.

Perhaps she wasn't quite as good a housekeeper as she might have been, and that annoyed him. Now she is gone and he remembers only his criticisms. He comes home at night and sadly says to himself, "I would willingly have everything out of place if only I had her back." He is haunted by remorse, by regret, by the memory of little complaints he made.

I told him that where his wife is now, in the greatness and vastness of the eternal life, these little things do not matter. All that matters is the greatness of her love for him. If she could, she would tell him so. I warned him that if he does not learn to forget, then the heavy burden of regret will deteriorate him. She lived her life. She knew that he loved her... For this man the future of his life depends upon whether he can put these regrets in the past and go forward.

Repeatedly in personal counseling one encounters this tragic inability of people to forget. A curious case is that of a man who cannot write when he gets nervous. When he goes to a hotel to register, his fingers refuse to function. He says that he deliberately goes to the end of the line so that everybody may register ahead of him. He dos not want anybody to see him make "this awful signature," with fingers that do not function properly.

I suggested that he go to a hotel, get at the head of the line, and in a loud voice that everybody in the lobby could hear shout, "Gather 'round, gather 'round, see the worst signature in the United States." That might help free him from this crippling inhibition. To overcome the nervousness of his fingers, he must break a long line of memory that goes back to the past, to childhood.

When he was a small boy, his father suffered a muscular accident that destroyed the ability of his fingers to write. The father became horribly self-conscious about it. He told the boy about it so often and so impressed it upon the boy's mind, that although there was, of course, no organic injury to the boy's fingers, there was what amounted to an injury to the mind. Long memory reaches out and puts its inhibitions on the fingers of the boy, now a man. It is a startling illustration of how a deeply held thought reaching far back in memory can render a man ineffective.

But it is necessary to develop skill in the art of forgetting. I have emphasized that the Bible is the wisest of all Books. The Bible contains the formula for forgetting: "This one thing I do, forgetting those things which are behind, and reaching forth unto those things which are before, I press toward the mark..." (Philippians 3:13-14). This formula contains the secret of how to forget and go ahead

"This one thing I do." The man who said this was resolutely disciplining his thoughts and controlling them. At the precise minute a man determines to control his thoughts, he is on the way to self-mastery. Usually our thoughts control us. The first step in forgetting is the simple determination to forget; to turn your back on something by reaching out to the things that lie ahead. Practice that thought pattern and you can break the hold of unhappy memory.

Mrs. Peale was at a meeting out on the plains of the West,

representing one of the denominational boards of your church, of which she was president. People came from miles around to this meeting, and all stayed for a church dinner. There had been a drought and much privation among the farmers of the plains. She sat across the table from a hard bitten, old North Dakota farmer—a shy man with big, rough hands. She tried to interest him in conversation but he did not respond.

So finally she asked him, "How are the crops this year?"

"The crops, well, I guess there aren't any crops this year," he replied.

She asked, "How is that?"

"Well," he said, "first we had grasshoppers—they ate up nearly everything. Then came a dust storm that destroyed what was left. But I was lucky. I got in five per cent of my crop, but my brother, who lives near me didn't get in anything."

The devastation was so awful that she sat awestruck and finally asked. "How do you feel about that?"

"Oh," said he, "I don't think about it any more. You see—I aimed to forget it."

This farmer had not enjoyed the benefit of the schools or other advantages, but for years he had gone to a little church on the plains. The winds swept against it, the snow piled deep around it in winter. It was seared by the heat of the summer, and the rains of the spring and the autumn beat against it. It had rough, wooden benches and old worn hymn books, but there he heard some very wise words, "This one thing I do, forgetting those things which are behind, I press toward the mark." The old man had found it a solid philosophy in disciplining the mind. He "aimed to forget." He may have lost that one crop but he saved himself.

Of course, some people can do that by force of will, but most people are not endowed with any tremendous power of will. It is very difficult to eject a thought by merely saying, "Be gone." Often such an attempt only tends to fix a thought more firmly in the mind. One must be more subtle. The secret is to substitute thoughts. *Expel one thought by substituting a more powerful thought.*

I have had some interesting correspondence with a doctor in the Midwest. He uses his religion soundly and skillfully in the practice of medicine. He told me about the ailments of some of his patients (no names, of course) and asked, "As a spiritual doctor, what would you prescribe in these various cases?"

He has one patient whose employer was unjust to him and dishonest as well. The doctor is satisfied that the facts are true and that the employer is as represented—cruel, unkind, dishonest, although he stays within the limits of legality. As a result of his ill-will toward the employer, the patient developed a peptic ulcer. The doctor says the ulcer is primarily caused by his disturbed state of mind. The hate thoughts, the revenge thoughts, the ill-will thoughts have made him sick.

He says, "The problem is to change the patient's thoughts if the ulcer is to be cured." The patient must change his thinking about his employer. He must stop secreting the poison of resentment. I cited the case of another man who became miserable through being resentful of people. One day he was reading the bible and saw the statement. "Vengeance is mine, I will repay, saith the Lord." "Well," he said, "if the Lord is willing to bother about these resentments, I will let him take care of this man who has mistreated me. The minute I shifted the responsibility of getting even with the fellow over to the Lord, and off my shoulders, I felt a hundred per cent better."

The Lord, in due time, will indeed "take care" of the person who has mistreated you. Why not follow this good advice and let God handle the matter? Do not waste your time in carrying thoughts of ill will toward somebody, because those thoughts do not hurt that somebody; they hurt only you. They may give you peptic ulcers.

Oftentimes a person will agitate you in order to annoy you. Knowing that you are annoyed, he is happy or at least thinks he is. I advised the doctor that he suggest to his patient this idea about mentally shifting the responsibility of resentment over to God. I suggested further that he persuade his patient to try the most subtle form of retaliation: namely, that he pray for the man who had mistreated him and thus set spiritual forces flowing back toward him; in short, conquer him by love. This is the most scientific of all reactions to an ill-will situation. As you affirm goodwill toward an enemy your mind will tend to forget and so gain relief. Shift this emphasis of the mind and master the art of forgetting.

Long held grudges, deep seated hates, form impenetrable obstacles to the flow of power through a personality. It is difficult to eliminate ill-will with its poisonous effects from the mind by merely being willing to do so. It is not quite that simple in the case of an habitual mental attitude.

The secret, as indicated, is to use a reverse method. Try to pray for the person you do not like. I realize that this may almost seem hypocritical, though it is not, but it is a method that will work. In so doing, you are setting against the corrosive effect of a grudge the only force more powerful than hate, namely, good-will or love. Long established poisons secreted by ill-will are dissipated by the curative force of good will.

Even the striving, however feebly, after an attitude of good will toward another person helps one to forget mistreatment. Many people are ruining their efficiency, making themselves miserable and in fact destroying any possibility of a happy future, simply because they will not forget insults, slights, or unfairness.

A man came to me with the complaint that "he simply had to get some peace inside of him." He could not sleep nights. He was nervous and tense. He snapped at people. Naturally, everybody steered clear of him.

In our church clinic we went over his attitudes, his daily schedule, and his general practices of thought and action. All checked well except one thing. He had what amounted to almost a hatred for certain competitors in his particular business. It happened that most of these men were of another race and religion and there was some prejudice mixed up in the matter, but mostly it was merely personal conflict, jealousy, ill will and unforgiveness.

I assured him he could be cured if he would follow the spiritual prescription I would give him. He replied that he would follow it, but almost broke his promise when the prescription was outlined. "For the next two weeks," I said, "you are to pray twice a day for each of your competitors by name. You are not to pray for yourself at all during this period. You are to pray that each of these men shall do a bigger business this year than you do."

"Why," he shouted, "That would be a big lie."

"Not in the mind of your true self," I replied.

You must get rid of the attitude of mind that is defeating you," I said. "You must learn to forget, and the only way to do it is to pray yourself into good-will if the poisons of ill-will are to be eliminated."

Grudgingly he promised to carry out this procedure, and he did. He reported afterward that for the first week it was a very painful process

"Imagine it," he said, "my praying and asking that those good-for-nothing high binders should go past me in business. But what do you know! As I kept at it, one day when I was praying, of a sudden I felt better inside. I felt light as a feather and happy and experienced such relief as you have no idea."

"The pain that was inside of you, has it left you?" I asked

"Yes," he replied, "It was just like a great wave of peace coming into me."

Now, months later, he tells me that he has even learned to like the men he formerly hated. He had a block that was causing a lessening of power in his mind. Had he kept on with this hatred, he would probably have become a sick man. Many people would find if they would honestly trace it back in their minds that much of their nervousness, irritability, even physical ills are caused by personal conflict and hate that they will not forget. In the instance of this man, his emotional sickness was healed by employing a powerful spiritual antidote, and as a result he became happy and efficient. He learned to forget and so he was able to go ahead.

One should not only "forget those things which are behind," but also "reach forth unto those things that are before." There should always be the idea of forward moving—moving away from a situation which one desires to forget. I know a wealthy widow, a gracious and lovely lady. Like many women bereft of brilliant business husbands and trusting people's honesty and kindness, she was fleeced out of a large sum. She lost thousands of dollars, and futilely she asked again and again, "Why did I do it?"

She had to learn to think of her experience as money well spent, for she learned a lesson. "It is worth fifty thousand dollars to you to learn that all kinds of people exist in the world, so take your lesson and walk away from it a wiser woman," I commented. Walk away from things that are over and past and cannot be helped. Reach forth to the things that are before. Take your lesson—make yourself wiser. Avoid useless post-mortems on past mistakes. Forget them and go ahead.

My friend, Grove Patterson, Editor of the *Toledo Blade*, and one of the greatest editors in America, says that he was a frequent victim of his own post-mortems. He would lie awake nights trying to figure out why he did this or that, or didn't do it. But he found a solution. Not being able to do anything about it, he just forgot it by saying. "So what!" This, says Grove Patterson, induces a strange tranquility. Of course it does, for it relieves the mind of the foolishness of carrying past actions which for good or ill are done.

Whatever has happened, it makes no difference what, there are only two things to do: (1) do everything that you reasonably can about it; (2) then practice forgetting it. Walk away from it in your thoughts. Conceive of it as lying back there growing ever more dim against the horizon as each day carries you farther from it. Unless you do this you will hamper your efficiency. If in addition to present problems, you pile high on your memory past actions that are now outdated, you will go staggering through life under an impossible load.

A high-ranking Army officer came to my office. He paced the floor, he wept. He was a big, fine looking man, and he apologized for weeping. I went out of the room and said "Go ahead, cry it out." When I returned he said, "My life is ruined."

He had been drinking considerably

"I tried to forget it by drinking," he explained, "but couldn't so I went out and got into a taxi and said to the driver, 'Take me to a church.' "

"What church?" the taxi driver asked.

"Any church," the officer replied.

"Catholic or Protestant?" asked the driver.

"Protestant preferably, but any church, take me to a house of God," was the man's reply. And the taxi driver brought him to our church.

"Well," I asked, "what is the matter?"

"I was never cut out for this military business," he explained. "I hate it with all my heart. I am a farmer and all my life I have loved growing things, I love life. I hate the destructiveness of war. I have seen it all, I have been through the most terrible experiences, things I shall never be able to forget," he replied.

"What is the main thing you won't forget?" I asked.

He replied, "One American soldier had shot another and I sat on the court and we voted him death. As long as I live I shall never cease to see the face of the kid, when one of his own American officers read the sentence that he was to die. I shall never forget his face."

This man obviously faced deterioration unless he could

properly learn the art of forgetting.

"You thought you did your duty, didn't you?" I said.

He replied, "Yes."

I continued, "The boy is dead, isn't he?"

"Yes," said he.

"You can't bring him back," I told him. "You as a representative of the sovereign rights of a nation passed judgment upon him. It was part of your duty as a soldier."

I said, "My friend, it is done. Why don't you look at that face that you say you will never cease to see and say, 'Son, I want to live for you as I live for myself, and in the long years that are to come, if there is anything wrong with the whole military system, I will do my utmost to correct it. I will live for your country and mine and the things for which you died.' "

The act had been irrevocable. He could not go back and restore the boy to life. This officer had to walk away from it, whether it was a mistake or not. The cure consisted of forgetting that which was past, and also of reaching forth unto the things that are before. He picked up his hat, there was a look of peace on his face and he said, "I see it. I have something greater than I realized to live for."

He asked and received forgiveness for any wrong done. Now he must forget the things that are behind, weave any mistakes into the pattern of life, discipline his thinking by bringing into the pattern of life, discipline his thinking by bringing into the mind spiritual thoughts of God's purpose, and walk away from the mistakes (if such they are), having learned wisdom from them.

My friend, Dr. Simley Blanton, an eminent psychiatrist, once stated to me that in his opinion the wisest psychiatric statement ever made was the words from Ephesians, "Having done all, stand." These words were uttered many generations ago by one of the most astute minds history has ever produced, a man named St. Paul. Dr. Blanton said that he has read practically everything in the field of psychiatry and that there is nothing to equal the wisdom and insight contained in these few words, "Having done all, stand."

The psychiatric, curative value of St. Paul's statement is based on the simple process—do the best you can. Do all you can. Give a proposition or a problem or a situation all the energy both physical and mental of which you are capable. Leave no stone unturned. Exercise all your ingenuity and efficiency, then realize there is nothing further that you can do about it; therefore, there is no use fretting, worrying or engaging in mental post-mortems; no use rehashing or going over the situation. You have done all you can do, therefore *stand;* that is, do not allow yourself to be upset, trust God and trust what you have done. It will come out the way it ought to come out if you will just leave it alone.

When Henry Ford was seventy-five years old, he was asked the secret of his health and calm spirit. "Three rules," he answered, "I do not eat too much; I do not worry too much; if I do my best, I believe that what happens, happens for the best."

The fact that religious people, that is, genuinely religious people, learn this art almost by second nature, is one of the reasons why the practice or religion is so vitally important.

I saw a very interesting and unforgettable demonstration of this truth in a railroad station in a large city during wartime. The gateman, a huge fellow, let some soldiers through the gate when the train came in before he allowed the civilians to pass through. A humble mother clung to a young soldier, to the boy's obvious embarrassment. She was making quite a demonstration of her grief, which apparently she was unable to control. The son gently, but firmly, was trying to get away from his mother, for unconsciously he realized that she was approaching hysteria. As he passed from sight through the gate, she sank against an iron rail and sobbed bitterly. Indeed, she all but screamed.

I was standing near by and noticed that as the crowd moved through the gate, the gateman was watching her closely.

Presently he left his post and went over and spoke to the woman. A change seemed to come over her as he talked. He assisted her to a seat. Her sobbing ceased and she leaned back, calm and relaxed. Then I heard him say, as he left her, "Remember now what I told you."

My curiosity aroused, I engaged him in conversation. "I watched you handle that woman, and if I am not too inquisitive, I would like to know what you said to her."

"Oh," he replied, "I didn't say anything."

"I am sure you must have said something very helpful," I coaxed, "for obviously it had its effect upon her. I would be interested in knowing just what you did tell her."

"Well, I will tell you. It is this way. I saw that she had lost her grip, so I just went over and said to her, 'Listen, Mother, I know exactly how you feel. I have been through it myself. Lots of people have, but you have just got to forget these things. I don't mean that you are going to forget the boy, but you are going to forget your fears.' Then I just added, 'Put your faith in God and He will see both you and the boy through.' "

A bit surprised, I asked him, "Are you a religious man?"
"What does it sound like?" he asked.

This man was wise in the ways of human nature because
he was a student of spiritual techniques. He realized that this
women needed to know how to forget her fears that she
might go ahead. He knew how to apply mental and spiritual
therapeutic. She, on the other hand, was able to receive his
guidance. In each of them faith was an active quality. Thus
the mental adjustment was made which gave her power to go
ahead. Her mind accepted the sane and sensible proposition
that "having done all" she could "stand."

Adversity and failure may become obsessions which freeze
the mind, thus preventing new ideas from gaining entrance.
One must be able to forget adversity and failure and go forward. If a person will keep his mind fluid, new insights and
ideas will come.

I know a man and his wife who discovered how to perform
this very important feat of forgetting in order to make progress.

This gentleman was a partner in a business which suffered
a disastrous fire and he emerged from this tragedy all but
ruined financially. It broke the spirit of both the man and
wife. The wife sat home and worried about it, and he went
out and worried about it, futilely tramping the streets. "Why
did this have to happen to us?" they bewailed again and
again. They simply could not forget it, and not only were
they failing to recoup but they were both getting into a highly
nervous state.

In fact, the wife worried so much that finally they sent her
off to a sanitarium. While she was in the sanitarium she
stumbled on a new idea of praying. She discovered that it is

not effective to pray frantically and in an attitude of desperation, for in so doing the mind is not receptive. Fear has closed it against any fresh concept. She learned to pray in a relaxed manner. She definitely practiced relaxing her body before beginning to pray. She relaxed her mind by giving the entire problem into the hands of God. In her prayer she said that she and her husband were ready to do anything that God wanted them to do, if He would show them.

After a few days her mind took a strange turn. She began to think of some pot holders she had made. The idea of these pot holders kept coming into her mind. They were simple little things made out of cloth, merely little pot holders that she had sewed herself. They constantly kept coming into her mind as she prayed. Finally in her prayer she said, "Lord, what is that you are trying to tell me about these pot holders?" She declares that the Lord seemed to say to her, "Go home and start making pot holders."

She felt this so keenly that she did go home and started making them. Her husband, a great giant of a fellow, sat in the kitchen and helped her. One day to his amazement he sold the whole lot of them to the purchasing agent of a chain store who said, "These are wonderful pot holders. We will take all you can make."

They went on making pot holders and then she thought of some other things to make. She was very handy. She began to make other little knickknacks which her husband sold to the store chain. To sum it up, they finally built a plant and at the present time have about four hundred employees making a great array of the most interesting and useful articles.

This woman's discovery of a new and simple technique of prayer did two things for her. First, it released her from failure by teaching her how to forget; and in the second place, having freed her mind of the creeping paralysis of this developing obsession about the past, she got an insight which changed everything and opened up a successful future.

This woman had to face a crisis. Usually we think of a crisis as a dangerous something that we wish we did not have to face. Perhaps when our civilization is older we may acquire some of the timeless wisdom of the East. The Chinese word for crisis has two characters. The first character means "danger." But the second character means "opportunity." And there you have it: a crisis is a danger point and an opportunity too. It all depends on whether you can forget the failures and mistakes and look expectantly to see in your situation, however unhappy it may be on the surface, the unexpected values and great opportunity it may contain.

Chapter Eight

HOW TO BE FREE FROM FEAR

"The commonest and subtlest of all human diseases is fear," says a distinguished physician.

A well-known psychologist declares that fear is the most disintegrating enemy of human personality.

Obviously these scientific men are referring not to normal but to abnormal fear. Normal fear is both necessary and desirable. It is a mechanism designed for our protection. Without normal fear a person cannot be a well-organized personality. He would be lacking in ordinary and sensible caution. Normal fear prevents us from taking chances, from doing hazardous and foolish things.

But the line of distinction between normal and abnormal fear is very finely drawn. Before one realizes, he may step across the line from normal fear into the dark and shadowy regions of abnormal fear. And what a terror abnormal fear is! It disturbs your days and haunts your nights. It is a center and source of complexes. It tangles the mind with obsessions. It draws off energies, destroys inner peace, blocks power. It reduces one to ineffectiveness and frustrates ambitions. Abnormal fear is the poisonous well out of which dismal unhappiness is drawn. It makes life literally a hell. Many are they who suffer from this grievous malady. How pathetic and pitiful they are—the unhappy victims of abnormal fear.

But you can be free from such fear. Abnormal fear can be cured. In this chapter we shall outline a cure that will work if you will work it.

A doctor, in boyhood, developed a fear psychosis. It grew upon him until by the time he entered medical school it was drawing off the energies of his mind so much that it was only by Herculean efforts that he was able to do his work. It put an abnormal strain on his energies which left him weak and ineffective.

With great expenditure of nervous energy he finally graduated and went into internship still carrying his heavy burden of fear.

Finally, unable to stand it longer he consulted one of his medical teachers and said, "I must be rid of this terrible burden of fear or I will have to give up." The older physician, a wise and kindly man, directed the young student to a Healer who, as he cleverly said, "keeps office in the New Testament."

"I followed my teacher's suggestion," he declared, " and that Physician gave me a medicine which made me well."

And what was this medicine? It was not a liquid in a bottle, nor was it compounded as a pellet, but it was in the form of words. It was that potent combination of words called Biblical text. "For God hath not given us the spirit of fear; but of power, and of love, and of a sound mind." (II Timothy 1:7.)

"I *took* those words," said the young doctor. "I allowed them to sink deeply into my mind. By a process of intellectual and spiritual osmosis, their healing potency penetrated and infiltrated into my mind and in due course delivery came, followed by a strange sense of peace."

It is remarkable what a few words can do when they are the right words. Dr. Edward Trudeau, famed pioneer in the treatment of tuberculosis, who himself succumbed to that disease, gained strength by repeating several times daily the word "acquiescence." He would say it slowly allowing its great meaning to sink deeply into his mind. Dr. Paul Dubois, Swiss psychotherapist, who had to struggle against obstacles, practiced saying the word "invulnerability."

I have observed the strange power in a similar use of Bible verses. The Bible advocates this practice, for it says, "If you abide in me, and my words abide in you, ye shall ask what ye will, and it shall be done unto you." (John 15:7.) That is to say, if a person *abides* (meaning a long-term, habitual, mental immersion) in communion with Christ, and allows Christ's words to *"abide"* (that is, to linger as a permanent thought in the mind), he will develop such a potentiality of power that life will flow toward him rather than away from him. He will be released and his powers function efficiently. Law then operates in his favor rather than against him, for now his changed thought pattern has put him in harmony with law or truth.

If you are troubled by fear, I suggest that you too "take" these healing words, "For God hath not given us the spirit of fear; but of power, and of love, and of a sound mind."

But what is the "medicine" that is compounded in these words? One of the words is *power*. What power? The only power that can counteract fear is the power of faith. Faith is ordinarily thought of as theological, as the acceptance of a creed. We also think of faith as an intellectual proposition, an assent to an idea. But there is another meaning to faith. It is something alive and active. It is a vital substance like sunlight, like the violet ray, like the growth of our beings. Faith is not only theological and intellectual, but also acts as a medicine. That is to say, it is a healing property for the mind, the soul, and often the body as well.

How is medicine taken? Ordinarily through the mouth or by injection into the blood stream, but there are other entrances through which medicine may be inserted. One is through the eye. For example, pick up the Bible and read some of its great words. A reflection is made on the retina of the eye. This image changes into the form of an idea: a positive idea of faith. The idea passes through the mind until it arrives at the infection point caused by fear. There it throws its healing influence around the center of infection. It drives off infection and finally through the therapeutic operation of a spiritual idea the diseased idea is cast from the mind. One, therefore, has taken medicine (a healing agent) through the reading of the Scriptures. A powerfully healthy idea has driven out an unhealthy idea.

Again, you may take spiritual medicine through the ear. Go to church. Hear the Bible read. Listen to the sermon. Sound waves fall upon your ear and are admitted into the brain in the form of a spiritual idea. By a similar process the healing idea makes its way to the diseased center and engages in battle with the fear thought. By reason of its superior power, faith drives fear out and takes possession.

The mind having been cleansed, the center of infection heals rapidly until a normal condition again prevails. This may be a curious way of describing the effect of faith in the mind, but this concept of faith as a vital healing agent has worked for so many that is validity is proven.

The world is filled with worried, anxious people, who are

made so because of the thoughts they habitually think. If such people will practice the creative idea of religious faith, allowing it to dominate their minds, everything can become different. Many people have been healed of the debilitating influence of fear through no other means than a new concept of faith entering their minds.

A prominent businessman came for an appointment. "Do you think I am losing my mind?" was his question.

"You look rational enough," I replied. "What makes you think you are losing your mind?"

"Because I cannot make the simplest decisions," he replied. "Throughout my business career I have handled matters of large importance and have made decisions affecting vast sums of money. But now the simplest and most seemingly unimportant decisions cause me no end of struggle. When finally I make a decision, I am haunted by the possibility I have decided incorrectly. As a result I am filled with fear. Perhaps my inability to make decisions is caused by my fear. Anyway I seem to be afraid of everything. I have been sitting in the balcony of your church on Sundays and am interested in the idea of faith as a healing property.

"Throughout my life when I have been sick physically, I have gone to doctors and they have given me prescriptions. Now I am not sick in my body, but I believe I certainly am sick emotionally and spiritually. I am slipping badly. Can't you give me a spiritual prescription?" he asked.

"Yes," I replied. "I can give you a spiritual prescription and if you will take it faithfully, you will get well."

"That is what I want," he said, "and I will faithfully practice it."

I gave him the following "prescription." When you

awaken in the morning before you arise, completely relax yourself. Stretch your arms out as far as possible, then allow them to fall limply on the bed. Do the same with your legs. Also practice opening and closing your eyes by letting your eyelids drop laxly. Relax your fingers. Then conceive of your entire body as being inert, yielded to the bed. Completely let go. Allow all the tension to go out of you. (This method of relaxation was more fully described in earlier chapters.)

When you feel that you have accomplished this, close your eyes and pray. "God, I am going to get up now and go to the office. You are going with me, for you said, 'I am with you always.' I shall not be afraid all day long because you are with me. I shall have some decisions to make, but you will be with me, and the decisions will be made satisfactorily because you will be there to guide me."

"Next," I said, "go to your office and after lunch lie down, if you have a place to do so. If not, lean forward on your desk. Put your head on your hands. Again relax the body and having done so, pray saying, 'Lord, we had a wonderful morning together. We made some decisions and they are good decisions because you were with me. We are forgetting them now and I am not afraid, for you are with me.'"

Finally, "Go to bed at a reasonable hour. Before you get into bed, throw up the windows, fill the room with fresh air, take a half-dozen deep breaths, inhale and exhale deeply, slowly. Deep breathing has a powerful effect in reducing tension. Then get into bed and again practice the formula of relaxation."

"What about saying my prayers? I always say them on my knees by my bed," he complained.

"Well," I replied, "evidently the kind of prayers you have

been saying on your knees haven't been doing you much good, so we will change the method of your prayers. I believe it is a good thing to kneel down to pray for the spirit of adoration is stimulated by the act of kneeling, but it is a mistake to become so stereotyped in your method of prayer that the freshness goes out of it. Try another method for awhile, if only for the sake of variety."

"That is wonderful," he said, "I always wanted to pray in bed but my wife would never let me because she said I would go to sleep before my prayers were finished."

"God would understand that," I said. "It isn't so much what you say as that you think of Him. He knows that is in your mind anyway.

"Get in bed and relax. Then close your eyes and pray, 'Lord, we had a great day together. I wasn't afraid because you were with me all day long. We made some decisions and they must be all right for you helped me make them. Now you will be with me in the darkness to watch over me. The decisions are made. We shall let them stand, and we shall have a great time tomorrow.'

"Then turn out the light and repeat these words. 'He giveth his beloved sleep." Then go to sleep. Don't be afraid of anything."

On a sheet of paper I wrote "Spiritual Prescription" and outlined the above described process. A man with a great brain has the ability to be simple. I have never seen a first class mind that could not be naive, simple, and even child-like. An intellect that cannot react simply is not a first-class mind no matter how profound a man may appear to be. This gentlemen had a first-class mind.

"Take that prescription three times a day for two weeks," I

said. "Then come back and see me."

Today he is a well man. His mind is clear. He is not afraid. He is in perfect control and is having the time of his life helping other people. He said he cannot understand how he lived so long and missed this "simple and wonderful secret."

Some time later I met an important executive of a large organization. He pulled from his pocket a little paper on which was written "Spiritual Prescription."

"Where did you get that?" I asked, and found that our friend had given it to him. This executive commented. "It worked for him and I was greatly impressed. It works for me also."

You do not need to be haunted by fear. Your religion can help you. It acts as a medicine, releasing power in your mind, the power of faith which drives away fear.

That the technique of faith eliminates fear many can testify. "The first time I jumped from a plane," a paratrooper told me, "everything in me resisted. All there was between death and me was a piece of cord and a little patch of silk, but when I actually found out for myself that the patch of silk would hold me, I had the most marvelous feeling of exultation in all my life. I wasn't afraid of anything and the release from fear filled me with exquisite delight. I really did not want to come down; I was actually happy."

Fear defeats us because we are unwilling to put our trust in what we regard as an ethereal thing, namely, faith in God, but like the paratrooper, when we leap out, trusting to faith, we find that this mystic and apparently fragile thing actually holds up up.

This is an important truth but I must confess that it took

me years to learn it and even longer to be willing to practice it. Strange how we can have at hand the formula that can mean so much, yet we will not take this attitude: "I will do all that I can do about any problem. Beyond that I shall trust in God and know my faith will hold me up."

The second ingredient in the medicine against fear is love. Love is one of the most misunderstood and misused words in the English language. Hollywood and current fiction have made of it a sticky, even questionable sentiment. It has been made synonymous with sex. But love is not that at all. It is a strong, dominant, curative emotion or force. It is the power by which we make transference to other people and through which they help us. It is also the power by which we make transference to God, through which God loving us, gives us strength and power. "Perfect love casteth out fear," because perfect love is complete trust.

Love is the natural, naive, basic relation that a human being should have with God. When he does, he can move through this world unafraid. He believes that someone is with him who loves him. He knows that he can trust this someone to protect him and watch over him.

If you really want to know how to live, associate with children. If you have none of your own, borrow some. There are times when I would almost be willing to lend you my three, but I would want them back very quickly, for I would become very stodgy without them.

When our first child arrived, I was afraid to touch her, thinking she would break to pieces. I know now that they are not as fragile as they seem and have been convinced that a little rough treatment helps them. I was not quite so fearful of our second child. He was a little tougher than his older sister, but it was not until our third baby came that I was really released.

I found great pleasure in tossing her high in the air. I did not toss her so far that I couldn't catch her, but she always seemed to enjoy being tossed. As I threw her up, she would take a breath, and then as she came down, she would snuggle into my arms and laugh like a rippling brook, and then cry, "Do it again, Daddy." I became amazed by the fact that apparently she had no fear. Children are said to have two basic fears, fear of falling and fear of loud noises, but she had no fear of being tossed. I think it was because instinctively she knew that the person tossing her loved her; therefore she trusted him. "Perfect love casteth out all fear" in her, so she yielded herself to the fun and was perfectly relaxed.

One of the wisest things ever said was when Jesus Christ advised us to have the attitude and mind of little children. Our so-called "smart" sophistication had just about ruined us emotionally. It may be one reason for the tension, "nerves," and breakdowns of our time. Form a simple love for God as a kindly Father who will take care of you. If you learn to love Him, you will learn to trust Him and then you will not say to yourself with terror, "I wonder what is going to happen? How will I ever get through this thing?" Trust God, believing He will see you through. This is a simple dogma of Christianity but it is one of the most neglected and unused. Develop a simple childlike trust in God and see how your problem of fear clears up.

It might be a good idea in church to take up not one collection, but two. Very large baskets might be used for the second collection, the ushers bringing them down the aisles.

The people might be asked to put not money but their fears in these baskets. When all the fears had been gathered up, let the ushers bring these baskets to the altar. They would be so heavy now that the ushers would stagger under them, but what sense of release would be in that congregation! Only one song could be appropriately sung, "Praise God from whom all blessings flow." The released congregation would sing with such fervor that the very roof would tremble.

But do you know what would happen after the benediction? The people would start out and then one by one with sheepish grin they would turn and come back to the basket in which each had placed his fear and fish around until he had found it. People are so used to their fears that they would feel homesick without them. People become such victims of fear that they are afraid to walk away from them.

But when a man habitually affirms, "I love God, He has been good to me and I can trust Him, so I am going to put my fear in His hands and walk away from it," that man will find release.

If you are worrying about something, practice this little formula before you start out tomorrow morning. Stop for a minute and say, "God is with me. He loves me. I can trust Him. So I will do my best and I won't be afraid." You can depend upon this to work, after you have practiced it for a few days. Make this an automatic procedure and it will release a tremendous power against fear in your personality.

The final ingredient in the medicine for the cure of fear is a "sound mind." Obviously the reason we have fears is because we develop an unsound or tangled mind. The unsound mind develops in various ways. It often begins in childhood when parents unconsciously implant their own fears and anxieties in the child's mind.

It also develops from the breakdown of morals so widely prevalent today. People get the idea that the Christian moral code no longer prevails and that they may violate it with impunity. They learn to their sorrow that what we call sin is, in reality a wound in the mind. Sorrow, for example, is a clean wound. It hurts, it cuts deeply, but it will heal because there is no infection in it. But sin is an unclean wound. It is a foreign substance invading the mind and the mind tries to close around it but it cannot; it becomes infected.

A man may carry this guilt through youthful years and even into middle life, but all the time like a suppurating tooth, it sends infection into his emotional system. Men will sometimes break down and attribute the disaster to overwork and it may be that, but often the real cause may the infection-drain of a sense of guilt. Out of this state of infection rise the ghosts which haunt a man's mind. These ghosts fill him with fear and his mind becomes so tangled with obsessive notions, reactions and impulses that everything is tinctured with fear.

It is really a very pathetic thing when one allows a foreign substance to enter one's mind. If you were to open up a fine watch and push a pebble into the works, people would think you were demented. Yet people do an equally destructive thing to their minds. It has got so that if anyone tries to dissuade people from committing this offense against themselves, he is termed an old fogy or mossback.

I have observed over a period of years in the religio-psychologio clinic of our church that a very large number who come to us for treatment are people afflicted with a sense of guilt. It is curious how many of those who come are on the young side of life, that is, under forty. Fear is their main trouble. Often the basic cause is that having departed from moral living they have become victims of a sense of guilt. The end of the process is such a tangle of emotional reactions that St. Paul's implication of an unsound mind is not far from the facts.

They are afraid that they will be found out. They are afraid of the future. They have lost confidence in themselves. They are afraid of other people. They have become victims of blind, unreasoning, fundamental fear. They have a psychosis. They throw the lie right back in the face of the unsophisticated novice in life who tells them that they must be "emancipated." There is only one way to be emancipated and that is through the discipline of spiritual morality. Follow that and you will not be afraid of man nor the devil. Your mind will be sound, stable and rational.

How is the "unsound mind" cured? Analysis often-times is helpful. When you understand why you react in a certain way, improvement often begins at once. Self-knowledge leads to self-improvement. The practice of spiritual formulae is helpful. One of the great needs is for people to know the "how" of practicing the spiritual life. People are urged to pray, but are not told exactly how to pray. We are urged to have faith, but are not instructed in the precise and workable procedures of faith. Our forefathers worked out techniques which were satisfactory to them. We need now to relearn the simple ABC's of how to put the curative principles of faith into operation.

In an attempt to meet this need the following incidents may serve as a suggested practice. These represent two simple "spiritual devices" which were employed successfully in the cases of two people who appealed for help...

There came to our church clinic a successful New York businessman who was haunted by fear. The strain was breaking him down, and he knew that he must find a cure for his fears.

He had started attending church, which he had not done for a long time. Then he came for an interview. He described attitudes and actions which certainly had infection qualities in them. He thoroughly cleansed his mind by confession. He received forgiveness, but his fears had continued for so long that he could not let them go. God had forgiven him, but he had difficulty forgiving himself.

He called upon me about every fortnight. I told him there was nothing to be afraid of. He would leave with his mind at rest, but two weeks later the fears would return and he would be back again. I finally said to him, "You fail to get rid of this state of fear because you are always asking God to remove it, yet not believing that He is doing so. You are an expert asker, but a poor receiver. What good do you accomplish by asking continuously, yet never practicing the art of receiving?"

I quoted the Bible statement, "Ask and ye shall receive, seek and ye shall find; knock, and it shall be opened unto you." I pointed out that the word "receive" quickly follows the word "ask"; that the word "find" follows hard upon the word "seek" and "shall be opened" comes closely after the word "knock."

The plain meaning, I explained, is that we are to ask, then have such simple faith that we shall immediately receive.

Here is a clear law: have faith, ask God for something,

believe that you will receive it. My caller said that he understood, but had never done it that way.

Then we hit upon a device. I asked him to put his watch on the table before him and, keeping his eyes on the watch, to pray for two minutes, asking God to take his fear away. He objected, "How can I pray with my eyes open?"

"Do you always pray with your eyes shut?" I asked.

"Certainly."

"Well," I observed, "your prayers with your eyes shut apparently haven't done you much good. Don't be stereotyped. Try praying with your eyes open."

Rather sheepishly he kept his eyes on his watch and for two minutes asked God to remove his fears. When the two minutes were up, he said, "Amen."

"Now," I directed, "say another prayer for two minutes, but this time thank God for doing what you asked: namely, for taking your fear away."

"Why!" he exclaimed. "Has He taken my fear away?"

"You asked Him to, didn't you?" I said. "According to the formula, your fear is gone—if you will let it go. You must make up your mind to accept the great thing God has done for you. So, for the next two minutes thank Him."

This was three years ago. Recently I saw the man again. "I'm away ahead of you," he boasted. "Nowadays I ask God for only one-half minute to help in solving a problem; and I thank Him for three and one-half minutes."

"Do you still use the watch?" I asked in surprise.

"Of course! You told me to, didn't you?"

The watch was merely a symbol, I explained. Symbol or no symbol, he said that he was going to "stick to the watch." I may add that those who doubt this as good religious practice might recall the Biblical injunction, "*Watch* and pray."

If you do not find help in your usual religious practices why not try such a simple formula as I have described? Simplicity is the essence of spiritual power.

A second incident illustrating spiritual techniques for the elimination of fear is the story of a young woman who telephoned me one day during wartime. Her husband was overseas, and so sure was she that something would happen to him that she had a bad case of nerves amounting almost to panic. She was in New York, away from relatives and friends; having no one else to turn to, she appealed to me as a minister. "What shall I do?" she kept repeating. "It would kill me to lose my husband."

"How old are you, young lady?" I asked over the telephone.

"Twenty-six."

I thought I heard a child's voice, so I asked, "Have you a youngster there?"

"Yes, a two-year-old girl," she replied.

"Is she upset and worried like yourself?"

"Why, of course not!" she answered.

"How do you explain her lack of nervousness?" I asked.

She hesitated. "Why, because she's only a baby. Besides, she has me, her mother, with her. I suppose she just puts her trust in me and lets me do the worrying."

That gave me an opening to suggest one of the simplest cures the Christian faith offers for worry. "Have you an easy chair close by?" I asked.

"If so, please draw it up to the telephone and sit down."

After a moment she reported that she had done so.

"Now put your head back," I directed. "Relax your body

and take three deep breaths."

For the first time, she laughed a bit, then asked dubiously, "Shall I really?"

"I suppose it does sound queer," I admitted, "but three deep breaths taken in and completely exhaled relieve tension."

"Next," I continued, after she told me she had followed these directions, "take your little girl on your lap. Now, make a transference; try to think of yourself as a child in relationship to God. As your child puts her trust in you, her mother, so may you, by concentrating upon it, put your trust in your Heavenly Father. Put your husband—put all three of you—in God's care. practice this simple procedure until peace comes to your mind."

She promised. After church the following Sunday a young woman came up to me and said, "I'm the one who telephoned you about being nervous. I tried your method, and it works. I have control of myself now and I know I won't get panicky again."

Then she added, "I always thought religion was a vague sort of thing—just something you believe in. I'm beginning to see that it really works."

Don't settle down to live permanently with your fear. If you do so you will never be happy. You will never be effective. There will be no success and happiness for you. Remember there is a cure for fear. Say confidently to yourself, "Through God's help and the application of simple techniques, I will be free from fear." Believe that—practice it and it will be so.

Chapter Nine

HOW POWER AND EFFICIENCY CAN BE YOURS

Every normal person wants a feeling of power. Not power over other people, for that is a disease and abnormality. But every normal person wants power over circumstances; power over situations; power over fear; power over weakness; power over themselves. And...everyone can have that power.

Everyone desires to be efficient; everyone desires to perform with skill. Efficiency is an element in power. Without it there can be no grip or mastery. There is great satisfaction in being able to do a thing well. To see a game played well, to hear a song sung expertly, to watch a skillful actor on the stage, is a source of happiness. It is not so much the game itself, or the song, or the action on the stage. It is the delight in witnessing a perfect demonstration. Even a commonplace thing done well gives a glow of satisfaction not only to the person who performs it but to all who witness it. This truth was recently brought home to me at a luncheon.

The service was by an old-fashioned butler, a master at his art. He had composure, a quality which is always to be admired. He was not in the least flustered as the average waiter or waitress seems to be these days. He took his job in his stride deftly and with gentility. Lingering after the luncheon, I said, "I want to congratulate you. I always like to watch a man who knows how to do his job. I admire the master of any art and I have seen one today in you."

He was pleased and said, "Beg your pardon, sir, it *is* an art. I learned it in England, sir, in the old days."

Let us take it for granted you want, like this superb butler, to be efficient. You can be efficient! How? Upon the answer depends to a large degree your success and happiness. And the answer is—seek to become expert in the practice of your religious faith. There was a time when a reader at this point would explain, "Here is where we go from common sense to theory." There is an old and false notion happily disappearing in this country that anything religious is theoretical—that it just doesn't fit into practical life. But intelligent people nowadays realize that Christianity is not a Sunday-go-to-meeting thing, remote from practical living, but a scientific, usable technique.

A prominent advertising man said to me, "There will be a definite upsurge of religion in the postwar era."

"Why?" I asked.

"Because," he replied, "after every great war, perhaps due to the dislocations incidental to war and the necessary readjustments, there is always a widespread desire for self-improvement. The best ways to improve yourself are by the application of either psychology or religion, perhaps by both of them. Psychology, in my opinion, however, does not go deeply enough; therefore this postwar generation will learn that efficiency, the ability to handle people and to get along, the ability to do things well, is a product of practical religion."

This advertising expert went on to tell about a large account that he had handled for several years. It was a course in beauty culture for women, which he had prepared by employing outstanding authorities to write booklets on various phases of the subject. One pamphlet told how to take care of the body; another how to eat properly; another how to use cosmetic preparations. The course was designed to release the inner charm and beauty of the feminine personality. This course together with a kit of cosmetic articles had been sold to more than a quarter of a million persons. Now a new advertising project had come his way, and he was discussing it with me.

The new project was to teach men how to be effective. The client was a clothing house, and a series of pamphlets was under preparation, each teaching a man how to be his full self and completely release his personality. For example, a famous athletic director was writing a pamphlet on exercise. Another expert was writing on how to wear clothes properly—how to know what shirt goes with a certain suit, and how to select a well-matched tie. Another pamphlet had to do with methods for approaching a customer, how to sell one's self, how to sell a product.

But the crux of the matter, said the advertising man, "is to teach our customers how to think; how to release the deeper spiritual self."

He concluded with this pregnant statement, "It is impossible to create an efficient man unless he has some kind of spiritual experience. Without this experience the thing that gives him the final touch of power is lacking."

There was a time when Christianity was generally regarded by the average person as theoretical and having no relation to practical everyday affairs. The advertising expert I have quoted is the refutation of this notion. Men who really think now know that Christian principles are the most skillful, most necessary principles in developing successful and efficient men and women. it is being demonstrated that no other system is so completely designed to give skill, power and efficiency to modern people as the simple principles of the Bible.

Here is further proof. A prominent periodical wrote up the "amazing" career of a successful business woman. What made her success all the more remarkable was the fact that she had had no previous business experience. So she had been asked to outline the principles upon which she had built her business. When she submitted the article, the publisher exclaimed, "This is astounding. These ideas are unique. Would you mind telling me where you got them?"

She smiled and said, "I guess you are not very familiar with the Bible. My article is practically a rewrite of the twelfth chapter of Matthew, verses 20-26."

The most antiquated man in America is the rare gentleman who still gets off the old canard that religion is something for Sunday only. That remark stamps him as belonging to the horse-and-buggy era.

Probably the reason so-called practical men think of Christianity as theoretical is because they regard it entirely as theology or philosophy. It does fulfil itself in these fields, but Christianity may also be thought of as a science. In fact, it is an exact science, for it is based on law as is any science. It is the science of personal and social living. Learn its laws and you will always and invariably get equivalent results.

It is rather crude to think that the only law existing in our universe is that which governs material things. We are constantly finding new applications of power in the universe and each new one is, as are all the others, regulated by law. The latest, of course, is atomic power. The average man scarcely knew this form of power existed, yet it has released such force that he is aghast. It is interesting to recall that years ago the famous scientist, Steinmetz, said that the greatest scientists of the future would be those who would chart and explain spiritual laws.

The New Testament has always been regarded as a distinctly religious book and it is that, but it may also be thought of as a formula book of spiritual science. It contains procedures by which anybody who intelligently applies them can develop power in his mind and personality.

So we have available a spiritual science equally as great, perhaps greater, and more valuable than the laws of chemistry, physics, electronics or atomics. In a power plant an eminent engineer once described to me a powerful dynamo. He commented on the amount of energy this dynamo could generate, but as we walked away he said, "It may sound queer, but you and I can generate more actual energy by means of faith and prayer than that dynamo can produce. I mean that too," he added firmly.

It is a fact that Christianity is a power mechanism. St. Mark says:

For verily I say unto you, That whosoever shall say unto this mountain be thou removed, and be thou cast into the sea; and shall not doubt in his heart, but shall believe that those things which he saith shall come to pass; he shall have whatsoever he saith.

Therefore I say unto you. What things soever ye desire,

when ye pray, believe that ye receive them, and ye shall have them.

Putting those words into the present-day speech, what do they say? Just this—if you have faith, not a great deal of faith, just a little real faith, not any larger than a grain of mustard seed, which is quite small, then you shall say to "this mountain," that great rock-like obstruction that lies across your pathway, always defeating you, "be removed," and it shall not only be removed, but shall be cast into the sea (i.e., swallowed up out of sight). And if you shall not doubt this in your heart—that is, shall not have a negative attitude about it in the subconscious—but shall simply believe, whatsoever you ask shall come to pass.

A psychiatrist of undisputed standing stated that one of the most powerful forces is released through a formula in Matthew which reads, "All things, whatsoever ye shall ask in prayer, believing, ye shall receive." He offered it as his opinion, based on long experience in his profession, that when a patient's mind is conditioned in terms of this scriptural verse, the most amazing changes can and do take place. "Faith," he said, "possesses a tremendous healing property and power producing force."

Regarding such passages from the Bible as those which I have indicated and others, there are various attitudes you can take. You may say, "I don't believe it, it is just not so." Of course, you have a right not to believe it, but it is doubtful if you have a right to dogmatically assert it is not so. In so doing you are setting yourself against the most reliable ancient document known to mankind. It forces us to take a choice between whether to believe you or the document. In the face of the religious belief of many distinguished men of science, the dogmatic statement that the Bible is not so is both unimpressive and unconvincing.

Another attitude one can fall into is a passive one. You may say, "I do not understand it, I do not disbelieve it, but it is beyond me and therefore I will not use it." That, of course, simply means that a person does not avail himself of power he could employ.

Probably the most sensible attitude is to assume that maybe it is true; that perhaps here is a law not perfectly understood, but one which many people have demonstrated will work. Perhaps it is wise to accept the workability of the law, deriving from it what power and efficiency one can gain, hoping later to penetrate into a deeper understanding. Matters of religion should be approached in the experimental attitude of a real scientist.

I spent an afternoon not long ago in the home and laboratory of the late Thomas A. Edison. Mrs. Edison showed me mementos of the distinguished inventor, unquestionably one of the greatest geniuses of all time.

Mrs. Edison said to me that after World War I, Mr. Edison told her that in the next war the great lack would be rubber. He stated that the chances were that our rubber supply would be imperiled, if not cut off—which revealed astounding foresight in itself. Realizing that it would be important to develop domestic sources of rubber, Edison began his experiments. In his painstaking and thorough manner, he examined innumerable plants in the hope of finding rubber. Finally he gave orders to his associates to take sickles and go out in the New Jersey meadows and cut down all the plant varieties they could find. The specimens were laid on tables and painstakingly examined one by one. Finally Edison discovered in the well-known and commonplace goldenrod the latex which he was seeking. At first he produced five per cent of rubber, later ten per cent, and then fifteen per cent. This was the experiment upon which he was working just before his death. When death interrupted his labors, he had released rubber from the goldenrod up to the point of fifteen per cent.

The lesson to be drawn from the example of Edison is this. Some people approach spiritual laws with the rational and factual attitude of the scientist and find at first a small percentage of truth which results in a degree of power. Those who keep on operating the law, investigating and working with it, increase the percentage and as they do so, there is released into their lives mentally, physically and spiritually an increasing power and efficiency which gives them a grasp and mastery far beyond other people, especially beyond those who just dogmatically assert, "There is nothing to it."

Years ago Emerson said there are unexplored chambers of the human mind which some day will be opened to release unrealized spiritual powers. A French psychiatrist says that there is another element present in the mind beyond the conscious and the subconscious. This element he terms "the superconscious." The characterization is interesting. Perhaps it was to this "superconscious" that Christ referred when He said, "If you have faith...nothing shall be impossible unto you." When His disciples commented upon the greatness of the works which He was doing, He said, "Greater works than these shall ye do." We read that "He marveled because of their unbelief." That is to say, He was astonished that people who had such potential power would not release it. It is entirely likely that in you is locked up all the power and efficiency you need. Evidence gained in thousands of cases indicates that the only sure way of releasing it is to become expert in the faith mechanism described in the New Testament.

Captain Eddie Rickenbacker discovered this principle years ago. He himself told me about his discovery. In an automobile race he was coming down the home stretch with his throttle wide open. Due to his sensitive "feel" of the mechanical workings of his automobile, he became aware that something was wrong. At the rate of speed at which he was traveling, this might spell disaster. He says, "A momentary tremor of fear crossed my mind, but... I lifted up my mind." He relates that a feeling of exultation passed through him. It was an overwhelming and absolute conviction that he could bring that machine in, not by his hands, but by the power of his mind.

He doesn't say this boastfully, but explains that at the time he told nobody of it for fear nobody would understand. Today, however, Captain Rickenbacker explains we are better acquainted with the law of psychokinetics, the power of the human mind over conditions, circumstances, material things. Indomitable mastery and control over adversity or opposition is exercised by the mind when the driving energy of faith is released.

I am confident of the scientific workability of faith in developing power and efficiency, for the same reason that any scientist knows that a formula will work, namely, he sees it work and gets results.

In my scientific laboratory (the Marble Collegiate Church

of New York) we had a member, a business executive, who became enthusiastically convinced of the techniques of faith. He had not been a long established church man and became interested in the church only because he was "sold" on the idea of Christianity and its formula of faith. "I think you have got something there," he declared. Because as he put it, "there is something to it," he joined the church and was regular in attendance, enthusiastically practicing spiritual techniques.

One afternoon he telephoned saying, "I must see you right away about an important business matter." One might think it curious that a businessman would see a minister about a business problem, but when you get right down to it, most business problems are problems in which persons are involved. The minister deals with persons and therefore he can be a scientific adjunct to anybody interested in business research.

My friend, who represented a specialized business in New York, came in and said, "Here is my problem. We have a competitor in the middle-west and this competitor employs the star sales executive of our industry. This man has forgotten more about the business than the rest of us know about it. Our competitor has discharged him, however, for the third and last time. I would like to employ him."

"Why don't you?" I said.

"Because," he replied, "there is a catch to it—he is an alcoholic. My president won't take him on because he says there is no hope for an alcoholic. I have continued to urge my president, however, because I believe we can cure him. I have heard you talk from the pulpit about faith and I am sold on the idea that if we have faith, nothing is impossible, so I have finally convinced my president, and he has told me he will give me one month to get this man cured and if we do, I can have him on my sales force."

"Do you realize what you ask?" I said, and then I explained to him what the scientific authorities say about alcoholism. I showed him that it is scientifically regarded as a disease, one of the most serious that can attack a human being, the usual end of which is either the insane asylum or death, or both.

"I don't know anything about that," my friend insisted. "I only know that the Bible says that if you have faith—'nothing is impossible unto you.' I take that as meaning alcoholism also," he concluded firmly.

"Does this man go to church?" I asked.

"No," he answered, "he doesn't. Not very often at least."

It so happened that a church supper was scheduled for a night or two later and I asked if he thought the alcoholic would come to that supper.

"Yes, I think he would," my friend replied. "I know he eats."

So I met this man. Later the alcoholic came to my office. He said, "Now listen, Doctor, Mr. V. is very much interested in me. He is an awfully nice fellow. But don't waste your time on me. There's no use trying to do anything with me. This thing has got me. I'm licked, completely licked."

He told me he was forty-five, and had two boys and a lovely wife. He had an engaging personality and a brilliant mind.

"You say you are licked?" I asked him.

"Yes, absolutely—completely washed up," he said.

"That's marvelous," I replied, "You are sure that you have

no strength of your own?"

"No, I'm all through. Sometimes I feel if I could only get free, if I only could...the things I could do! But the minute I think I am free, drink knocks me back and it has knocked me back too many times. Don't waste your time on me."

"My friend," I said, "when you tell me that you have no strength of your own, you are at the beginning of deliverance, because now you are ready to say, 'Having no strength of my own, I put my life in the hands of God with faith.' In so doing you will get strength, all you need."

"Do you think I have a chance?" He looked up with wistful eyes.

"Yes, I certainly do."

"All right," he said, "I'll do whatever you say. What do you want me to do?"

"Let's start," I suggested, "by your going to church twice every Sunday for the next month."

"Oh!" he groaned; but he agreed to do so.

I wrote to Mr. V. as follows:

Yesterday I had a very satisfactory talk with Mr. C. Our discussion was exceedingly frank.

I found him absolutely honest, and it pleased me that while he admitted his weakness and did not seek in any sense to minimize it or hide it, at the same time he was not unduly derogatory of himself. Sometimes there is a tendency for a man to run himself down completely, which means that his self-respect has run out. He simply, honestly, faced with me the great weakness of his character, and convinced me that it is his definite purpose to eradicate drinking from his practice.

He told me that he has made one discovery which he would never admit before—namely, heretofore he has gone a considerable period of time without drinking, but always believed that he could take one drink and control the matter at that point. Now, he says, he has learned that he must not drink at all, that one drink inevitably leads to more. This is pleasing, because it is extremely difficult to get an alcoholic to the acceptance of the fact that he must not drink at all. The biggest delusion in the mind of the alcoholic is that he can drink moderately. With men who are alcoholically inclined there is no such thing as moderation. Therefore I believe that real progress has been made with this man. He stated that his contact with religion had not been very close, but that now he has seen that religion can be a practical power in a man's life, and agreed to follow certain ideas which I laid down to him and which he found in my books. He also is going to associate himself with Alcoholics Anonymous.

I believe he has definitely started up the road which leads to complete sobriety. I have weighed this carefully and I would not give this as my opinion unless I felt that he honestly means business. I think he does, and I assure you that I shall do all in my power to help him.

Incidentally, I think you have used extremely good judgment and common sense in the way you have approached this matter.

The next Sunday morning I looked down and there was my friend, Mr. V., on the end of the aisle. Next to him was the alcoholic, and then Mr. V.'s wife. Mr. V. came up after the first service and said, "Now, Doctor, for a while forget about the rest of the congregation and preach to this man.

We have to get him cured. I need him in my business."

I confess that I almost did. He was there regularly, listening carefully. It was very impressive: two businessmen trying to settle a business problem as a human problem.

One Sunday night about three weeks later, I was preaching on the text, "What things soever ye desire, when ye pray, believe that ye receive them, and ye shall have them," and outlining the power of affirmative faith. I found myself saying, "If there is anybody in this great congregation defeated by anything, no matter what it may be, if he will now believe that the power of God is being released in his life and if he will, as our heads are bowed, raise his hand as a sign and symbol of his acceptance of this power, I declare that he will now receive it"...which was an astounding thing to say, but I said it. We would get more astounding results from Christianity if we were not timorous about believing in it.

About fifty hands went up all over the congregation. To my astonishment I saw this man's hand go up. After the service this man came up to me, shook my hand, and went away, but indirectly I heard he was doing well. Later he told me that when he put up his hand "something happened to him." A feeling came over him such as a man experiences when after a long illness suddenly he realizes that he is well. The urge to drink did not come back. The desire *completely passed away.*

To complete this narrative, I insert the correspondence that documents this working partnership of business and religion in the problem of alcoholism.

From letter of Mr. V. written to me:

I know you are interested in Mr. C. and of developments

in connection with our program together.

I was unusually impressed and gratified to receive a letter from Mrs. C. which has reference to Mr. C. and I am sure you will be happy to read some extracts from it, and so I quote them below:

"He certainly is a changed man and I am sure it is due in a large measure to contacts with you and members of your family. I do my very best to keep up the good work while he is home. He is so sincere it is very easy to do. I've gone to church all my life and have brought the boys up that way too—but Mr. C. certainly taught me a great deal about the power of faith and I'm very grateful."

You can imagine how thrilled I was to get this word from the wife of this alcoholic and my delight in the success attendant upon our efforts was increased when I received the following letter from Mr. C.:

I know you will be interested in the success that has rewarded our efforts of the past several months. The final result is my appointment as General Manager of the ——— Company. At the next meeting of the Directors of the Company I am to be elected Vice President, also.

Nothing approaching this was contemplated at the outset. The sequence of things that led to it, even now, seems unbelievable. I am indeed awed. They didn't just happen and certainly were far beyond my planning. I know He answered my prayers, and yours, also those of Mr. and Mrs. V., and Mrs. C. Even my two youngest boys, ages eight and ten, included in their nightly prayers 'Special prayer for Daddy.'

But better than all this I now have a firm hold on myself. I am sure I have the complete and simple faith to which you refer in your books and sermons. My mind is at rest and I know peace and happiness again. You can readily appreciate what it means to my wife and three boys. It has been no effort to avoid my old weakness. I seem to have found a substitute—faith.

I find it difficult to adequately express my gratitude. The change dates from the time I first attended your church and had the opportunity to talk to you personally. Then the high spot that Sunday night in your church when on your suggestion I raised my hand in the way of public acknowledgement of God and put myself in His care. To me that was tremendously impressive.

Many problems will be facing me—perhaps the biggest in my business experience. I approach them with complete confidence and with the knowledge that unlimited power and help are always available to me.

When I received this letter I knew that a healing had taken place. Even as medical science is able to develop an immunity against certain forms of disease, so it is possible by the application of spiritual techniques to change emotional and mental reactions so that a person becomes as the New Testament so picturesquely expresses it "a new creature: old things are passed away; behold, all things are become new."

So I wrote to Mr. C.:

You have found the secret; by faith you have accepted God's power and He has given it to you.

May I suggest that you form habits of prayer in which you constantly affirm to God that He has given you this strength, and thank Him for it. Pray not only in the morning and the evening, but get in the habit of turning your mind to God frequently during the day. Also, I suggest that you form the habit of reading the Psalms in the Old Testament and Matthew, Mark, Luke and John in the New Testament. Read a chapter every day if possible. These suggestions are to build up in your mind a consciousness of God's presence and His power. This is part of a definite spiritual technique which is very valuable.

This story of the alcoholic goes from one climax to another. A year and a half later in one of my letters I told him that I never failed to pray for him and that I was very much interested in having reports from him from time to time. To this suggestion he wrote me the following tremendous statement of his experience.

I am humbly grateful because you still remember me in your prayers. It is my firm conviction that that has helped me through very difficult situations. I am referring to the many problems of business today, not my old difficulty. That is a closed book. It is now a year and a half since I even had a drop of intoxicating drink. It has not even been at all difficult. Surprisingly enough, I have never once been tempted. I am confident I won't be. This just could not have been if I had not attended Marble Collegiate Church, met you and had that first talk with you. You pointed the way that changed everything for the better. My spiritual highlight was in your church one Sunday night when the congregation sat with heads bowed and eyes closed and I responded with others in raising my hand, putting myself unreservedly in God's hands. All of this is written in complete sincerity.

At the end of a year and a half he declared that he had *never even been tempted to drink alcohol*, that the cure was still operative.

Nearing the end of two years, he called on me in my office. He told me that he was on his way to the middle-west where his company had recalled him and had made him Vice-President for the Dominion of Canada. As he sat across from my desk I asked him, "Have you ever had the desire to take alcohol since that night?"

His answer was, "Not the slightest desire."

Some people might call this a miracle. Anybody who knows the true meaning of the disease of alcoholism is well aware of the astonishing thing which happened in this case.

However great a recovery this is, it is not a miracle. This man had made contact with a spiritual law. He was changed by the operation of this law. He discovered a basic power in the universe just as truly as the man who released atomic energy. This power is so great that it burned out of his mind every vestige of the disease which was destroying him. He discovered and put into operation the law of faith.

But the story goes on and arrives at one of the great factors in the cure of alcoholism; the urge to help someone else get cured. Mr. C. writes:

I have a purchasing agent with plenty of the very same difficulty I had. I have been trying to help him over a period of several months with considerable but not complete success. I have talked to him many times—got him going to church—given him many of your sermons and books to read, and have tried to pray for him regularly. So far I haven't been completely successful in convincing him that he can't do it for himself but to let God do it for him.

You can still feel proud of the job you did on me. It is fast approaching three years now since I have had a drink. I am much safer than any man who never touched a drop. But beyond that and more important, you showed me the way to build religious faith and trust that means more to me than all else. I have a long, long way to go but I really believe I make some little gain each day. In a very humble way I try to help others do the same. You know it is rather convincing to others when an old sinner like myself tries to show the way.

I do not relate this story on the supposition that you, the reader, are an alcoholic. My purpose in telling this story is to point out that if faith can revitalize and remake an alcoholic, it can assuredly give you power and efficiency.

All around you at this moment is divine healing energy. The very atmosphere is charged with it. If you will practice faith, you can be healed of ill-will, inferiority, fear, guilt, or any other block which impedes the flow of recreative energy. Power and efficiently are available to you if you will believe.

Chapter Ten

HOW TO AVOID GETTING UPSET

"That fellow burns me up." The speaker was flushed of face as his fist crashed on the table. "I'm sick of that fellow's name in the newspaper. I'm all burned up inside."

That's a picturesque and exact description of the inward condition of that man. A seething cauldron of agitated emotion, he was truly burning up on the inside. A human being cannot forever stand resurgence of such agitation. Every day we hear of people who become ineffective or "break" and in many cases it is simply because they allow people or situations to "burn them up."

One important rule for being happy and successful is— don't let things agitate you. This is vital.

A doctor once told me what he had prescribed for a businessman who complained that his nerves were "all frazzled." "You don't need to be agitated or upset. Practice your religious faith," he suggested.

"Do you get many such cases, and is that your usual prescription?" I asked.

"Yes," he replied, "I have noted a pronounced rise in the number of emotional and nervous problems. Many patients become ill simply because of inability to overcome prolonged agitation. But, except in cases where a definite physical cause exists, my belief is that the average person need not be agitated or nervous if he will take the medicine you parsons hand out."

This wasn't the first time this idea had been presented to me. About twenty years ago I took my mother to a prominent heart specialist in Boston. After a thorough examination he leaned back in his chair and looked quizzically at my mother and said, "Mrs. Peale, are you a Christian?"

My mother had been a minister's wife for a good many years and an active church worker. This question startled her.

"I try to be," she replied.

"I am afraid you are not working at it very hard," the doctor said, "and there is very little I can do for you. I could prescribe some medicine but beyond palliative effects, I honestly do not believe it would be of value. I suggest that you definitely practice the technique of trust, calmness and faith which you find in the New Testament. Do that and I think you will get along all right," he said.

Today we know that an important step toward emotional and physical health is to believe in and practice your religion. Religion contributes to physical and emotional health because it deals with mental states and attitudes. Many human ills, as explained many times in this book, derive from improper thinking.

A physician stated recently that whereas twenty-five years ago only two per cent of stomach disorders, indigestion and affiliated maladies were traceable to mental states, now probably twenty-five per cent of such cases are due to nervous tension or agitation. People get sick largely because they cannot control and discipline their minds.

People often say that their nerves are "all shot to pieces." This is usually not so; very seldom are their nerves actually damaged. The nerve is simply a telephone wire from the brain to a given part of the body. What a person means when he says that his nerves are "all shot to pieces" is not that there is anything wrong with the actual nerve, but that the thoughts which stimulate the nerve are disturbed. These agitated thoughts make it impossible for the brain to send orderly and controlled impulses to the nerves so that contrary and uncertain messages go out over the nerve wires. The brain is in confusion because the thoughts are in confusion. Thus the nervous system tends to be in disorder. As a result one feels nervous, tense, tied-up and agitated.

Nervousness is primarily derived from the thoughts we think. Learn to think orderly, controlled, disciplined, calm thoughts and you will not be tense or agitated. In view of these facts it is more and more evident that the chief cure for the prevailing tension and agitation of this era is a return to religion.

I met a friend, a minister, whom I have not seen in several years. I had heard that he had suffered a nervous breakdown. But now he seemed robust and looked the picture of health. We sat in his library one winter day before a cheerful fire. He stretched out his long legs, leaned back in his chair and asked, "Have you ever given thought to the relationship of religion to the art of resting? Our religion," he continued, "has been so concerned with morals and ethics, both matters of the greatest importance, that many have failed to realize the tonic effect of faith. Why," he exclaimed, "it is amazing what religion can do to cure tension, heal worried and anxious thoughts, and give strength for the stresses and strains so prevalent today."

"You must have found something," I prodded him.

"I surely have. A couple of years ago I had a nervous breakdown. I went to a hospital and was put through all the tests. My energy had gone. I was weak and listless. Finally the doctor in charge of my case gave me his diagnosis." (It was an experience not unlike that of my mother's previously described.)

"We have analyzed your case, Reverend Doctor So and So," he said, "and we have decided that if you practiced Christianity, you could get well." Astonished, my friend demanded, "What do you mean?"

"I suppose you never read the New Testament," continued the doctor.

"Of course, I do," protested the minister.

"Oh, I see," pursued the doctor. "You read it but you do not belief it."

"I do believe it," shouted the minister.

"Well, then let's put it another way—and come now, admit it—you don't really practice its teaching of faith and trust, do you? I know you practice its morals and ethics, but you do not practice your religion in your thought life. Put into mental practice these principles: 'Take no thought for the morrow' or 'Let not your heart be troubled'—'Fret not thyself'—'Come unto me, all you that labor and are heavy laden, and I will give you rest.' "

It began to dawn on my friend what this wise and kindly doctor meant. Quietly he said, "I see what you mean and you are right. I will practice my faith in my thoughts as well as in my actions."

"It's really a great medicine—the greatest tonic of all," said the physician.

There sat my friend that day of our visit, two years later,

well and strong. His wife who sat by smiled and said, "I told him that for years, but he would not pay attention to me but went on wearing himself out and becoming a bundle of nerves."

"Well, I'm cured all right," he continued, "and now I'm urging people to practice the gospel for the sure release it will give from tension and fear. I urge them to take the greatest medicine of all."

A friend of mine, manager of one of the largest hotels in America, had been commenting upon what he said this country needs, namely, "to get back to the simple principles of religion."

"Why," he said, "if we don't do it everybody is going to crack up. I move about in the lobby of this hotel a good deal and one learns a lot just by watching people. All you have to do is just to stand and watch people use the revolving doors and you will see what I mean. Why, for some men the whole day is spoiled if they miss one section of that door."

"You mean it annoys them to miss one complete revolution of the door," I remonstrated.

"No, sir," he said, "it used to be that but now they are so tense, it upsets them to miss just one section. Something must be done or we are all going to be nervous wrecks."

The results of such tension are clearly evident. Pick up any newspaper any day and count the causes of the deaths reported. Also observe the age at which men die. If you get past fifty today you may live to a ripe old age. High blood pressure, heart failure, maladies of hypertension, these are the sickles that the old man with the long beard uses to cut men down in their prime these days.

It is understandable how men break under strain. In the

manufacturing of automobiles the severest test is to drive the car at high speed over a smooth concrete pavement. It would seem that the toughest test would be over a rough road, but on the contrary, high speed over smooth pavement sets up high frequency vibration which more quickly indicates hidden weaknesses. High tension and agitation in a human being vibrate those hidden weaknesses which cause him to break.

Caruso had a dinner trick which used to delight his fellow diners. He would hold aloft between his thumb and forefinger a fragile glass with a long stem. He would sing the ascending scale and sound a high note repeatedly. The glass would shatter into a hundred pieces.

If high frequency vibration or tension thus affects an automobile or a glass, think what it can also do to our highly organized human personalities and bodies.

In his book, *Release from Nervous Tension*,* Dr. David Fink explains the process. He calls attention to "the interbrain." "Nerves," he says, "control all of our organs. These nerves are grouped chiefly in one part of the nervous system, and this part of the nervous system is the central control that normally should keep our hearts and stomachs and lungs working in harmony with each other. This nervous center of our emotional life is called the interbrain. Sometimes it is called the thalamus or hypothalamus. The interbrain is the seat of the emotions: love, hate, fear, rage, jealousy, etc."

---

*David Fink, *Release from Nervous Tension* (New York: Simon and Schuster, Inc., 1943).

Dr. Fink quotes Dr. Harvey Cushing as stating that "emotional storms coming out of the interbrain can cause ulcers of the stomach, palpitation of the heart and other maladies."

The interbrain, says Dr. Fink, "sits in the driver's seat." He explains its working. "Above the interbrain is the forebrain, sometimes called the cerebrum. The forebrain which occupies most of the space within your skull is the part of your nervous system that analyzes, thinks, decides. It lets you know just what is going on in the world. It is with your forebrain that you read a newspaper. Your forebrain interprets the general situation and sends its findings to the interbrain for action and feeling. The interbrain reports the situation back to the forebrain in terms of elation or depression. When you feel calm or happy or sad or depressed, or when you have the jitters or nervous indigestion, you know it because your interbrain has told your forebrain just how it feels."

Dr. Fink sums up, "To enjoy good health you must first get right with your interbrain."

Perhaps a man who was sent to me by a physician was having interbrain trouble. Over the telephone this physician said, "I am sending a patient to see you. Physically there is nothing wrong with him. All he needs is to get his nerves converted." Perhaps he should have said, "He needs to get his interbrain converted." "Show him how to put his trust in God and he will not be so jittery and upset," concluded the doctor.

A diffused and general application of religion will not necessarily help to overcome tension. No reader should jump to the conclusion that if one goes to church next Sunday, all will be well. I certainly advocate going to church next Sunday and every Sunday, but it is essential to do more than sporadically rush into a church in a desperate manner. I know people who have gone to church for years who are still pathetic victims of tension and agitation. The failure lies in the fact that they have never learned how the simple and practical techniques of Christianity may be applied to tension and agitation.

A man who is sick doesn't rush into a medical library and start desperately reading. He sits down with the doctor. The doctor examines him and out of his knowledge of those medical books and long years of practice, writes the patient a prescription and gives simple advice to apply to his particular malady. The patient takes the prescription to the drug store. He does not think he will be cured by subjecting himself to the aroma of all the medicine in the store. The druggist fills the prescription, giving him a specific medicine. He writes specific instructions on the bottle or box—"Take three times a day as directed." Religious practice should follow similar procedures, diagnosis, and specific application of formulae.

A man came to our church clinic complaining of severe nervousness. He was a manufacturer and was under great stress. He drummed his fingers on my desk as he talked.

"Why are you drumming your fingers?" I asked.

"I didn't even know I was drumming them," he replied in some surprise.

"Well," I suggested, "don't drum your fingers. Just let your hand rest on the table in a limp and relaxed manner." I saw that he was sitting rigidly on the edge of his chair, so I urged, "Sit back and relax."

"In what other ways does your nervousness manifest itself?" I inquired.

"I worry about my business all the time. Every time I am away I worry whether my house is going to burn down or something happen to it. I worry about my wife and children, wondering if they are going to get hurt."

I gave him a prescription, a little formula to practice. "Just say to yourself, 'Let my house burn.' Is your house insured?" I asked.

"Yes, it is."

"Well," I continued, "say to yourself, 'let it burn.' Also say, 'I put my wife and children in God's hands, He will take care of them.' You must learn a simple technique, you must have the naive genius to follow the greatest of all thinkers who told us that the answers to life's problems lie in childlike or simple attitudes."

He said, "I'll try."

"Good," I said. "Imagine that Jesus Christ is actually by your side. When you start worrying, stop and say, 'Lord, you are with me; everything is all right.' When you go into a restaurant even if you are with somebody, pull up a chair unostentatiously and imagine that Jesus Christ sits in that chair. When you walk down the street, imagine that you can hear His footfalls, feel His shoulders, see His face. When you retire at night, pull up a chair by the bed and imagine that Jesus Christ sits in that chair. Then before you turn out the light have a word with Him and say, 'Lord, I'll not worry, for I know that you are watching over me and will give me peace.' "

"Oh," he protested, "that sounds foolish."

"It is merely a simple psychological device to make you feel the presence of Christ and I have had a great many people use it with excellent results," I explained.

He came back to see me not long ago. He did not drum his fingers. He sat evenly in his chair, there was no nervousness. There was a new look on his face. "You feel better?" I suggested.

"Yes, I do; yes, I do." He hesitated, then said, "I should like to say something to you. You know that business about Christ sitting in chairs, and walking with me?"

I said that I recalled my advice.

"Well," he said rather hesitantly, "do you know I honestly believe there is something to it—I believe He is there actually."

He is right. There is something to it.

Another man who came to my office agreed with this finding. He told me that he could not sleep. He was quite haggard, and obviously at the breaking point.

"The trouble is my mind is too agile," he complained. His education was largely scientific, with degrees from an engineering school. He was a man of brilliant mentality, but his mind operated too rapidly for his emotional make-up and did not synchronize with his living.

This discrepancy in my visitor reminded me of the incident of the city man who went out to the country and watched a farmer who was sawing a log with long, even, measured strokes. This city fellow said impatiently, "Here, let me saw the log." He started in with slow, measured strokes, but before long accelerated the tempo. The stroke went crooked, the saw caught.

The city man said, "I guess I didn't do so well, after all."

The farmer replied, "It's because you allowed your mind to get ahead of the saw."

Tension causes men's minds to get ahead of their emotional nature—and dislocation of a perfectly synchronized and correlated personality results. That was true of the man who had come to see me.

I asked him to practice a simple spiritual device. "When you go home and go to bed tonight, put a chair by the side of your bed. Imagine that Christ sits in the chair, and when you get ready to go to sleep, look over toward the chair and say, 'He giveth his beloved sleep.' Then make it personal—'He giveth me (his beloved) sleep.' Believe that Christ will be there watching over you. Then turn out the light and go to sleep."

He said, "I'll try. But it's only imagination, because Christ couldn't be there."

"Try believing it just the same," I suggested.

He told me later that for the first four nights nothing happened, and he had just about decided it was a "crack-brained notion," as he put it. "But," he continued, "the fifth night I had a wonderful sleep. And," he paused, "I believe that Christ's presence is more than imagination—it is a fact."

The last time I saw him he said that he still puts the chair by the bed. Of course, he is resting too heavily upon the symbolism of the chair. But if he can get results by pulling up a chair, it's all right, for back of it is one of the most powerful, one of the most effective, one of the profoundest of all ideas, the idea, namely, that God is with you and that no harm can come to you, that you need not be afraid of anything.

The devices for eliminating agitation need not be involved. One is to practice taking a detached attitude toward irritating things. Practice lifting your mind above the confusion and irritation around you.

One way to do that is to form mental pictures of great hills or mountain ranges, or the wide sweep of the ocean, or of some great valley spreading out before you. Get a mental picture of the stars serene in the heavens, or of the moon sailing high on a clear, calm night. One can do this while busy at a job. Hang these pictures on the walls of your mind and think about them habitually.

The practice of detachment helps one to remain quiet, peaceful, controlled in the midst of the little tempests of this life. Let me tell you of a few people and the devices or techniques they have successfully employed to overcome agitation.

Just before Christmas one year my wife took me shopping. I always try to avoid it, but so far have never yet been able to get through a Christmas season without having to go shopping. She took me to a crowded store, and the counter where we wanted to purchase some articles was the most crowded of all. It was literally besieged by women. To my embarrassment I was the only man in the crowd.

I noticed the salesman. He was a tall, easy-going, young fellow who wore the button indicating honorable discharge from military service. He had a very relaxed attitude even though he was being called on all sides. He gave his attention to the one customer whom he was serving at the moment. It seemed that she had bought three articles, and I was standing close by when he tried to add up the cost. She had her eyes glued upon his pencil as he added the column, and you were conscious of a stiff and suspicious attitude on her part. Perhaps this confused him, for he added the column incorrectly, and I was struck by his wholesomeness when with a boyish grin he said, "What do you know? Didn't add it right, did I?"

"No, you didn't," she snapped. Dutifully he tried it again, appealing to me meanwhile to help him. Despite my clumsiness in mathematics, we managed this time to get the column correctly added.

Then he flashed her a radiant smile so warm that it thawed even the iciness in her face, and he handed her the package with the statement, "I am a poor mathematician, but believe me, you have got some fine articles there for Christmas. I hope they are going to make the people for whom you have bought them very happy. Merry Christmas!" And with that he turned to the next customer, who happened to be myself.

I discovered that he had been employed recently by a large advertising firm. Before putting him to work they sent him out, as he put it, "to get acquainted with the great American public." He certainly was in a place where he could get acquainted with the public all right and I asked, "How do you like it?"

"Oh," he said, "I like it all right; only why is everybody so mad? They storm around my counter from all directions, and they all seem to be mad. I don't know what they're mad about; I doubt that they know themselves. They are buying Christmas presents to make people happy, and yet they're all mad. But," he added, "I've got a secret; I just don't let it ruffle me. I flash a big smile on 'em and treat 'em nicely; it breaks them down—every last one of them."

This young fellow had hit upon a technique for not being

agitated. If he holds that throughout his life, he will be a successful man. He got relaxed, gave his attention to one customer at a time, and "flashed a big smile on 'em." In other words, he had mastered the skill of being detached. Thus irritation had no power over him.

Robert Louis Stevenson made a wise statement: "Quiet minds cannot be perplexed or frightened but go on in fortune or in misfortune at their own private pace like the ticking of a clock during a thunderstorm." That is really a discerning bit of wisdom.

I have a little old farmhouse in the country—a place over one hundred and fifty years old. We have some old things around the house, including clocks. There's something fascinating about the ticking of a clock, especially in the quiet of the night. One of those old clocks is in the dining room. One day we had a violent hurricane. The great maples seemed almost to bend double under the driving winds. The rain beat upon the windowpanes. The very beams of the house seemed to creak.

But the old clock acted as if there were no storm at all. "Tick tock, tick tock," it said calmly. If the clock had been a modern human being, it would have speeded up its tempo as if to cry excitedly, "Isn't it a terrible storm? What shall we do, what shall we do?" But the clock was measuring time which is rooted in the center of the stars. It was measuring decades, generations, eons, not merely excitable little minutes. So, it just went on, "at [its] own private pace."

A man who has cultivated "the peace of God which passeth all understanding," does not get agitated by the little storms of life. His life is rooted in something eternal so he goes on "at [his] own private pace like the ticking of a clock during a thunderstorm."

The late William Jennings Bryan, one of the greatest orators of our time, had this art perfected. Years ago a friend of mine was with Bryan all one summer. He slept with him in country hotels. He even slept with him on benches in country railroad stations. One night they lay down on a couple of baggage trucks somewhere in the Tennessee mountains as they waited for a train. At this time a certain newspaper was pounding Bryan unmercifully. My friend was wrought up about it. That night he said, "Mr. Bryan, why is it that you don't get worked up and mad and excited about the attacks this newspaper is making on you?"

"What newspaper?" asked Mr. Bryan.

"Why," said my friend, "don't you know?" And he named the paper.

"Oh, that one—well, you see, I never read the papers that attack me. I only read the others. The papers that attack me do not seem to me to be logical," concluded Bryan with a chuckle.

You may say Bryan's was a closed mind? Not at all. Bryan felt that he was right in the positions he was taking. He did his best and after that just went on "in fortune or in misfortune...like the ticking of a clock during a thunderstorm." Had he read the papers that attacked him and allowed himself to become irritated, the next thing he might have done would have been just what they wanted him to do. They wanted him to fight back angrily, knowing that "whom the gods would destroy, they first make mad." Bryan was a religious man. He had the peace of God inwardly. His enemies could not get him off center.

Gandhi also practices this formula. The seventy-five-year-old Indian nationalist leader said recently that he planned to live another fifty years. He said his plan to reach the age of a century and a quarter includes an abundance of humor, balanced diet, avoidance of all stimulants, adequate sleep, deliberate refusal to be annoyed, disturbed, angered or upset, resignation to the will of God, and prayers twice daily.

I have a friend, a public figure who is often attacked quite violently. He never shows agitation. "I don't understand you," I said to him one day. "I should think you would sometimes get disturbed because of what they say about you."

"It doesn't bother me," he said.

"Why not?" I asked.

"I have two never failing sources of peace," he replied. "One, the short stories of Tolstoy; the other, a Book known as the New Testament. Do you know," he said shrewdly, "it is a funny thing about this business of speaking unkind things, of speaking ill about a person. Point your finger at me," he said. I did so. "Now, what are the other three fingers doing? Pointing back at you, aren't they? You see I win three to one." Incidentally that is a good trick to employ the next time somebody says a mean thing about you. Somebody points one finger at you but three accusing fingers point back at him.

The person who is organized and calm and controlled in his mind by habitual practice of the formula of faith can live without tension. The secret is to develop the art of detachment, the ability to live above agitation.

One of the surest methods for overcoming agitation is to put yourself in contact with the re-creative process of nature. All nature is constantly being re-created. Every spring we see it demonstrated. The trees, flowers, and grass are attuned to the flow of that energy which is ever present in the earth. When a man is created, he is not set off by himself to run down like a clock that had been wound up. He is more like the electric clock which constantly rewinds itself by being connected with automatic and constant energy.

The process is described in one of the most astute and remarkable statements in the Bible, "In Him (that is, God) we live and move, and have our being." (Acts 17:28.) That is to say if you keep in continuous conscious contact with God in your thought and actions, you have life and energy and fullness of being.

This may be done by reminding yourself daily that "In Him I am living, in Him I am having new energy, in Him I am realizing the fullness of my own being."

Take time every day to affirm that the re-creative process is taking place in you, in your body, in your mind, and in your spirit. A new feeling of aliveness, eagerness, and vitality will come to you by following this simple practice.

A doctor telephoned me and said, "I have a patient for whom I can do no more. He thinks the wrong kind of thoughts. That is your field," the doctor concluded, "and if you will take him over, I will send him down."

I asked the doctor what he would suggest that I could do for his patient, and he answered, "Teach him to think differently. I suggest that you persuade him to commit scripture passages to memory until he fills his mind so full of these healing ideas that the other and destructive ideas are expelled. Of course, you know that you cannot force an idea out of the mind by being willing to do so, but only by putting in a stronger idea can you displace a thought that is causing damage."

I was impressed that an up-to-date physician would make such a simple and yet apparently wise suggestion and determined to try it with the man.

The patient was a resident of Westchester County and was engaged in business in New York City. He had "New Yorkitis," a disease that is a combination of anxiety, haste, tension and panic, all rolled in one. "New Yorkitis" literally shakes people to pieces. It is a product of the high tempo of metropolitan life, and thus not limited to New York City.

Every morning it was this man's habit to come into the city on the 8:29 train which he barely caught after dashing from his house at 8:28. On the train he read the paper, and got madder and madder at what he read. Before he was in the city, he was in a rage. In the evening he would go out on the 5:19, which he caught at 5:18^1/$_4$. Again he read the paper and again he got mad. As a result he was not far from the end of a pretty frayed rope.

He was disgusted when I suggested that the doctor and I both thought the cure lay in committing scripture passages to memory. "So you want me to go back to the primary department," he sneered.

"Yes," I said, "you may have some formal and ethical religion, but as far as knowing the simple techniques of applying the Christian faith you just don't know how, so we have to start you again with the ABC's."

I explained how our plan would supply new ideas and would gradually expel the agitated thoughts and spread a healing balm of peace and quietness through his mind.

He had a good brain and he got the idea; the simplicity and logic of it appealed to him. He agreed that he would carry out the "prescription." As suggested previously, a great mind has the capacity to be simple; in fact, a mind that cannot be simple is not a first-class brain. This is why the greatest Teacher said that if we want to become expert, we must "become as little children," that is, simple, naive, artless.

This man did as directed and one day about six months later the doctor telephoned and said, "Our patient is cured. He has control of himself now. His mental outlook is changed and he feels better in every way. I am again impressed by the amazing re-creative power of simple Christian practice."

Sometime later I made a speech in Buffalo before a large audience. It was a hot night and I spoke with vigor. Afterward I shook hands with several hundred people. A man tapped me on the shoulder and said that I had barely time to get my train. He rushed me through the city at "breakneck" speed, skidding around corners on two wheels, arriving finally with a great flourish in front of the Lackawanna Station, his brakes screeching.

Carrying two bags, I dashed through the gates which I heard clang behind me as the conductor called "All aboard." I threw my bags on the platform and pulled myself aboard as the train started. I was out of breath, panting and actually shaking. The car was crowded. There was no place to sit down, and the only thing to do was to get into my lower berth. Still highly keyed up from the experience of the preceding two hours, I lay in my berth.

Suddenly I became aware of a pain in my arm and around my shoulder. This disturbed me. Then it seemed that my heart was beating too fast. Foolishly I tried to take my pulse.

It appeared to be running about twenty beats to rapidly. The thought came that people die in Pullman berths and I thought, "Wouldn't it be terrible to die here in this berth?" A possible newspaper headline, "Minister dies in berth," flashed across my mind.

Then I remembered the suggestion that one could quiet oneself by reading. Unfortunately the only reading material I had was a book on the foreign policy of the United States which obviously was not designed to fill the mind with peace. Then it occurred to me that if the prescription I gave to the man from Westchester County worked for him, why wouldn't it work for me too? "Practice what you preach," I said to myself.

So I said quietly to myself a number of scripture passages. Then I recalled that some psychologist had said that it is more effective to verbalize aloud any statement designed to affect the mind, so I began to recite these scripture passages out loud. What the man in the upper berth thought of this, I do not know. But I lay there reciting all the scripture verses I could recall which dealt with quietness, peace, faith.

Presently I began to feel quieted. Drowsiness came over me, and a deep sense of rest seemed to spread throughout my entire body. The next thing I knew it was morning and I was in Hoboken. The route of the Lackawanna railroad is tortuous through the mountains of Pennsylvania, but I slept soundly and had to be awakened by the porter.

It was a rainy, dismal, raw morning, not designed to lift the spirit. However, as I stood at the prow of the ferry boat, crossing the river, I noticed the seagulls diving and gliding and it came over me that I had never seen such grace and beauty. I had never observed the loveliness of seagulls before, but now I thought I had never seen anything so exquisite as the graceful way in which the birds slipped down the wind. Suddenly it occurred to me that everything seemed wonderful and then I realized that I had never felt better in my life. I had a feeling of health, energy, vitality, and aliveness that was positively exhilarating. I felt deep happiness bubbling up. I caught myself saying, "It is wonderful to be alive," and I eagerly looked forward to the responsibilities of the day. As a matter of fact, I never had a better day in my life.

I became aware that unconsciously I had discovered a law, one of the greatest of all laws, namely, the formula for the re-creation of a human being through the practice of faith. It is a law that can revolutionize your life. It can make the whole world different because it can make you different.

Chapter Eleven

HOW TO ATTAIN MARRIED HAPPINESS

Happy married life is possible to those who will apply to themselves a few simple, common-sense principles. The "complications" said to destroy so many modern marriages are not inevitable. In truth, the marriage problem has often been made too involved by the "experts." I have counseled with married couples for a good many years at the heart of America's greatest city, and as a result I am convinced that many marriages which are at what seems a breaking point can be firmly and permanently held together by the application of the princples outlined in this chapter. These principles are not advanced as theoretical propositions. They are stated as the laboratory result of working with hundreds of couples in the confidential relation of a spiritual advisor.

The function of a counselor is not to consider the problems of dispute between a husband and wife and attempt to sagely settle them out of some superior wisdom. Even were he able to exercise perfect judgment and contribute the soundest possible advice, still in most cases, the cleavages which cause the dispute would remain. When a marriage comes to the point of serious disagreement, it probably cannot be settled entirely on the basis of logic or judicial discussion. Some positive treatment must be given to the basic causes which have thrust a husband and wife into warring camps, one against the other.

I am not much concerned about a moderate amount of disagreement or even bickering, for it is not unnatural that a certain amount of conflict should exist between human beings living in close proximity. I have never been impressed by the statement often made that a husband and wife have lived together for, let us say, forty years, and never had a cross word. Ignoring the question of whether the assertion is true, it still remains that it would be a rather dull existence for two people to live together on such an insipid plane that there never would be any argument. A good, robust difference of opinion strenuously engaged in is not bad for human beings provided they never let the sun go down on their wrath. If they carry over from one day to another accumulated irritations arising from personal disagreement, serious division may ultimately develop. Battle the issues out if you must but get them settled and forgive any sharpness before you go to sleep for the night. Let the passing of each day witness an unanimity of spirit, regardless of the divisions of opinion which may have occurred during the day.

While it is the custom of this day to rationalize most marriage failures on the basis that the partners were not by nature adjustable to one another, the fact remains that most could have adjusted had they taken the situation in hand and corrected a few simple faults. For example, one of the most basic drives in human nature is the craving to be appreciated. No less a person than William James so declares.

William James was one of the most distinguished scholars in American history. Considering the importance and extent of his works, he may be regarded one of the greatest minds to be developed on this continent. He was an eminent philosopher and was one of the early pioneers in the science of psychology. In one period of his life, William James had a long and protracted illness, in the course of which a friend sent him a potted azalea, together with words of personal appreciation. In making reply to his kindly gift, the distinguished philosopher-psychologist said it had reminded him of an immense omission of which he had found himself guilty in writing his immortal work on psychology. He had discovered to his chagrin that he had omitted from his textbook the deepest quality of human nature—namely, the craving to be appreciated.

Let husbands and wives get that fact fixed in their minds and never forget it. Indeed they should constantly remind themselves that *every person craves to be appreciated*. Govern yourself accordingly and you have nipped much married trouble at its root.

The husband who accomplishes some achievement in his business wants appreciation from his wife. When he has worked hard all day long and comes home tired, it is a serious mistake for his wife to take it all for granted. She should tell him how she appreciates him as a husband and as an individual. It is easy to say, "I'm proud of you." It will do wonders for him.

If the dinner is good, let the man appreciate it and *say so*. If it isn't good, do *not* say so but find something else to appreciate. Live in hope, it may be better next time. Think appreciation rather than criticism. If there has to be criticism, set up a family conference and get everything out on the table but don't snip and snarl and condemn and look askance. Do not develop the habit of seeing the things that are wrong. Condition your attention to the things that are right and appreciate them, *and say so*, and say so *often*. It will do her a world of good.

And now down to cases...

A young woman, obviously in great mental distress, came to consult me. She was seriously considering leaving her husband, she said.

From her story it soon developed that all she needed was a little ordinary appreciation. Some more profound authority might call it affection but to me it seemed simpler than that.

I talked with the husband who said, "Oh, she would never leave me."

"Don't be so sure of that," I said.

He looked stunned. "Why, she could not do that. What could I ever do without her?"

"Did you ever tell her that you couldn't do without her?" I asked.

"Why, no," he answered, "I don't like that kind of talk and besides she knows it anyway."

"She may know it, but she wants to have it told to her just the same."

"Why?" he said.

"Don't ask me why," I replied. "That is just the way of women." (But it isn't only women; all of us have the deep craving to be appreciated which William James spoke about.)

"Have you by any chance brought her flowers or candy lately?"

He was a huge, clumsy-looking fellow.

"Now, wouldn't I look fine lugging home flowers? I would look like a fool, me carrying flowers," he snorted.

"Just the same," I replied, "my professional prescription in this situation is to invest in some flowers and tell her you cannot get along without her."

Grudgingly he agreed to do it and, as it later proved, that attitude was all that was needed. It broke up the growing coolness between them, dissipated misunderstanding, and stimulated the original strong affection that basically existed between them.

I realize that this may appear to be oversimplification, and I am aware that in serious marriage disagreement, this may not be effective, but in the early stages simple appreciation is one of the most important of principles relating to married happiness.

Great issues develop from small beginnings. A lack of appreciation which reveals itself in commonplace things may grow until it becomes a very great divisive factor. It may even come to be an almost insurmountable barrier.

A case was brought to me by a wife who traveled several hundred miles to talk about her marriage which she said was crumbling. In fact, she and her husband had been living apart for some time, but there was sufficient desire on the part of both to hold the marriage together to cause them to agree to meet in New York and to visit our church clinic to lay their problems before us.

The couple were in their mid-thirties. Of good families, they were college graduates and were extraordinarily intelligent people. It developed that the man had engaged in several extra-marital affairs which he brazenly and rather cruelly described in the presence of his wife, since at that particular point I was seeing them together. He later attempted to impress me with the fact that one woman with whom he had developed what he called a "beautiful love affair" and whom he had described as a paragon of virtue, was, as he finally admitted, not quite so classic in her purity.

In private conversation with the husband I asked him to

be objective, to lay aside emotional reactions as far as possible, and tell me what he thought was the reason he and his wife first began to drift apart. To my astonishment he opened up a vigorous tirade against his wife on the basis of her alleged poor housekeeping, plus personal dowdiness. His complaint was that she did not think enough of him (that is, did not appreciate him enough) to properly care for the home. It seemed that she enjoyed going out with "the girls." These girls were her college friends and they had together developed a craze for bridge playing. It was their habit to gather in some convenient place for lunch and play all afternoon. This happened several afternoons each week.

Late in the afternoon she would dash home and throw together a few things, ending up with an obviously improvised dinner. Often the beds were not made until time to retire. The clutter which normally accumulates in a home was allowed to remain. This, he said, was more than he could stand. "I may be fussy, but when I come home, I think I have a right to find the place at least straightened up, a decent meal on the table and certainly the beds made."

Apparently he was a rather meticulous fellow. "Before I was married," he declared, "my bed was better made than after I married her." Moreover he complained, "Why in the name of heaven can't a woman keep her petticoat out of sight? It hangs down all the time."

While I sympathized with him and shared his views on both housekeeping and petticoats, I found it necessary to remind him that when he married this woman, he did not hire her as a housekeeper. I pointed out that he made a contract to live with her not as a man with a housekeeper but as a man with his wife, that they were supposed to become as one, sacred partners for life. I also pointed out that the two little boys had nothing to say about being brought into the world by him in partnership with his wife, and that he was simply the breaker of a contract, giving no thought to the two boys or to his own sacred agreement, but thinking only of his own comfort and nicety of his life.

The discussion revealed that he still had a strong attachment for his wife though there was considerable acidity in their relationship.

Later in talking with the wife I noticed that he was right, the petticoat did show. Her hair was rather frazzled. She was basically a nice-looking lady but no care had been exercised in her dress. I asked her if she liked housekeeping. Her answer left no room for doubt. "I positively hate it," she declared. One chief trouble with her husband was that he didn't make enough for her to have a maid, she complained.

I pointed out to her that when they were married, there was nothing in the marriage contract about her having a maid. Furthermore, I told her she was young enough to work hard in the home, and that hard work would do her good. I asked her if she went out with the "girls" and she said she "certainly did." I raised the question why once a week wouldn't be sufficient for her bridge parties with "the girls." I also politely suggested that she pull up her petticoat and that she make the beds the first thing after breakfast and pick up the newspapers and sweep the place out. I told her that while I was no housekeeper, still I knew that if she would budget her time and activities, she could do up the place in no time at all.

She wanted to know why a minister from whom she expected some spiritual counsel laid all this stress on how she fixed her hair, on why she didn't pull up her petticoat, and on being a better housekeeper. I replied that those matters seemed to be the trouble points.

He had a "few" deficiencies which he admitted and with which we dealt. The interviews ended by mutual pledges that the simple principle of appreciation would be applied and that these obvious deficiencies would be corrected.

Inasmuch as this chapter may be read by persons whose marriage has ended in divorce, I want to say something to help them adjust to that situation. Often such an experience may result in a severe shock to the personality. It can wreck one's life and totally blot out happiness. But there is an answer to even this tragic situation, as the young woman discovered who wrote the following very moving letter to the author.

I want to tell you that your book* has saved my life and reason, and brought Christ Jesus into my tortured brain and starved soul and breaking heart. I certainly needed Him as much as any other human being alive. You have also saved me from a nervous breakdown.

My background was religious, but when I got to college I dropped all interest in anything but the pleasures in this material world, and I guess I have been practically an atheist since, believing only in the Golden Rule. If I had only had a personal faith and lived by it I can see that my life would not have been in the turmoil that it has been.

When I was twenty-five I was married, happily for five years, and had one son—when I was thirty my husband deserted me spiritually for a young girl of nineteen—I tried for ten years to keep my home together, not knowing what else to do or where to turn—he stuck to her for five years, during

_____
*"The Art of Living"

which time I was so afraid of him I didn't dare make an issue of it. If I had only gone to a man of God who could have helped me! After that we never found each other, and hardly spoke, and in 1946 I was so exhausted with his mental cruelty that I gave up and got a divorce in order to save my brain and spirit.

Later I found out that he was engaged to this same girl, and in the flash of an eye all my old love came back—it was as if the agony of ten years didn't exist—and with my love came emotions of hatred, revenge, jealousy and rage—a sickening fear made me physically ill so that I couldn't eat or sleep, and I became weak and dizzy—by the fourteenth day I knew I would have to call a doctor, although I knew that a doctor couldn't cure my fear and breaking heart. I was pacing around the room, and said to my sister, "I've got to get some help from somewhere." On trying to get my mind off my terror I picked up a copy of your book—as I started to read, somehow I felt better—the chapter on fear helped me so much, and somehow all of a sudden I seemed to feel safe—and as if I wasn't alone—then like a rushing torrent it came over me—this is the answer—the blessed Lord Jesus— where have I been all these years of nightmare, fear, agony and destruction of spirit? Then I read your marvelous sentence, "Christianity is not a creed to be recited but a power to be tapped." And I remembered the Bible verse—"Fear thou not, for I am with thee." These two thoughts stayed with me, *power* and *reassurance*—I talked with my sister about it, and as I looked into her beautiful blue eyes, filled with love and compassion and tears, I knew I had found HIM.

After that I was able to eat and sleep, and while those dreadful thoughts of desire for murder, bitterness, grief and heartache kept coming back, I would look to heaven and keep my mind on Christ's love and sacrifice, and in the past month they have gradually disappeared. I have been praying constantly for grace and goodness, reading the Bible a great deal, and my mind is healed. Aside from that I feel that I have discovered something marvelous, which will sustain me through whatever life brings in time to come. And I see my husband, not as a heartless brute, but as an unhappy and desolate man, also looking for comfort and help all these years, and now trying to find it in another woman's arms instead of in the right place. This thought has helped to take away the bitterness, and left in its place a feeling of compassion, and a sincere wish for his happiness. I know that if he can ever find God he will come back to me, because we had a wonderful love, and we both love our son dearly. I have no way of helping him, except through prayer, as he is very bitter about the embarrassment of the divorce, and will not see me, but perhaps God will show him the way, if it be His *will*—if not I know I can carry on, and will be useful to my boy and others.

Another principle of basic importance in preserving married happiness is to decide how much you love your children. The husband of a famous Hollywood motion picture actress said to me when some of the press agents of Hollywood first suggested his wife's divorce, and I might say even instigated it (though without deliberate intent), that there could be no divorce because, he exclaimed, "we have the baby and can we cut the baby in two?"

His expression is well taken, for that is exactly what frequently happens to the children of a broken home. They are not cut in two physically but they often are emotionally. Out of a long experience in a religio-psychiatric clinic, I can state that many of the adults with whom I have worked on the matter of divided personality or inner conflicts, or haunting fear and inferiority attitudes, were made so because they were the children of broken marriages. Instead of selfishly thinking of themselves, let parents give thought to the future of their children. The sense of responsibility ought to have some weight with people of character. Perhaps if parents actually knew what their children think, it might help them to avoid some mistakes which wreck home life and cause agony. In the last analysis the children are of first and final importance to a man and wife; that is, if husband and wife are real people. When a child comes to a couple, he is of more importance than their own personal "happiness" (this word used in the Hollywood manner).

One day years ago a young boy came to see me. He was fourteen or fifteen, and was very nervous. He was on the verge of tears. As he clasped and unclasped his hands the blood came and went at his knuckles.

"I must talk to you," he blurted out. "I can't talk to my mother nor to my sister. I haven't anybody to talk to. I must talk to you."

"Go ahead, son, what is it?" I said. "You can talk to me. Tell me anything that is on your mind."

"Well," he said, with great hesitance, "I want to ask you—is—is—is my dad all right?"

"What do you mean, son, is your dad all right?"

"I mean," he stammered, "is he straight? What they say about him isn't so, is it? Please tell me the truth," he demanded.

"I admire your father very much. I do not know anything bad about him. What is on your mind?"

"Well," he said, "at school they kind of laugh at him and whisper—they have got him mixed up with some woman. Oh, gee, that isn't so, is it?"

The boy was obviously brokenhearted and suffering intense agony. So I said to him, 'I don't think so, son, but even if it is, you have to act like a man."

"Shall I tell my mother about it?" he asked, "or shall I go to my father?"

"No," I answered, "don't tell your mother and you can't talk to your father about a thing like that. Just pray for him and keep on believing in him. Keep on loving him and having faith in him."

I did nothing about it for a few days but it troubled me. I did not want to believe it either but I began to have my doubts, so I thought it was my duty to see this father. Naturally he was very angry and told me it was none of my business. That attitude I expected.

I said to him, "I only came to you because of this boy of yours. I just want to tell you how your boy feels." I told him of my interview with his son, and said, "You are going to lose this lad if you are not careful. Your name is being tossed about in a way that humiliates the boy. You can get mad at me all you please but I am just warning you. You had better give it some thought. Do you want the boy or the woman?"

He did not answer but sat at his desk, sullen, angry, face ashen, trying to control himself.

A few days later he came to me and said, "Well, I guess I had better get it off my chest. Yes, it is so. I really did not want to do it, but I did. Now I am in it and I am caught. I guess I'm a dirty dog and I hate myself. My wife is the finest woman in the world." Then he turned to me with a look of fear and almost fiercely said, "My boy doesn't believe this story, does he?"

"Not now," I answered, "because I told him it wasn't so. At the time I really did not think it was."

"Well," he answered, "what can we do about it? We've got to do something."

"There is only one thing you can do about it," I said, "and that is quit it; quit it right off. Break with it instantly and then decide to lead a different life. That is all. Just quit it and get straightened out."

One Sunday about six months later I received this family as members of the church. They stood in front of the altar, the father, mother, sister, and the boy. I do not know to this day how many of them ever knew the story. They never mentioned it to me, but I have never seen anybody happier than that boy that day. I can see his face yet as he stood there struggling to keep back tears, but his smile! It was like sunshine through rain.

That was years ago. The boy is grown up now and is a man in his own right. The sister is married and has her own family and the father and mother are at home alone but they are living together in deep happiness. Their hair is turning gray now, but strangely enough every happiness and joy and success has come to them. Theirs is a religious home and they are very proud of their boy and you should see how proud he is of them, especially of his father who obviously has always been and is now and ever shall be his idol. The boy has turned out to be a great success in life, a magnificent personality, but had that home broken up, I am convinced it would have broken him also. Marriages that break very frequently break the children, and there is no escaping this fact. One can never live that guilt down. It will haunt one in the subconscious mind. It will sour "happiness." It is something to think about as one strives toward married happiness. Think seriously about this matter and perhaps you can solve your differences.

As might be expected, this author believes that personal religion and religion in the home is the best of all answers to the problem of married happiness. The author is joined in this belief by psychiatrists, social workers, judges, and others whose occupations bring them into contact with marital problems.

And well we should be concerned for during the year 1945 there was one divorce for every three marriages in the United States. This compares with a rate of roughly one to six before World War II and one to nine just before World War I. In some communities there are now as many divorces as marriages.*

A Philadelphia newspaper recently carried a symposium on the alarming divorce situation. During the particular week under discussion the Marriage Bureau issued 533 marriage licenses, and for the same period the court handed down 236 divorce decrees. The newspaper stated, "You don't have to be a viewer-with-alarm to get excited over statistics like those. Something is happening to the sacred institution of matrimony, not only in Philadelphia but all over America, for the divorce rate is skyrocketing everywhere. Attribute it to post-war social upheaval, if you will, or blame it on Hollywood influence. The fact remains that an astounding number of couples today do not look upon marriage as the permanent affair our parents and grandparents did."

---

*The figures are by the Commission on Marriage and the Home and by the Executive Committee of the Federal Council of the Churches of Christ in America as quoted in *The Christian Advocate* for March 20, 1947.

The newspaper called upon two distinguished judges of the city, both of whom have passed on thousands of divorce cases, to express their opinion on the subject. After analyzing the various reasons for divorce, one judge said, "I blame it primarily on a lack of religion. Where there is no religion, there is no civic or social responsibility. Where there is no social responsibility, there is no family responsibility, and lacking that everything goes out of the window."

The other judge stated, "Overindulgence in alcoholic beverages is a cause of disagreement in a large percentage of divorce cases that come before my court."

Apparently also many businessmen hold the same opinion regarding the value of religion, first in preventing and second in settling marriage difficulties. The head of personnel of one of the largest businesses in America telephoned me one day saying, "I have a young man and his wife here in my office and I wonder if you would be good enough to talk with them. This young man," he explained, "has been working for our company as head of our branch office in another city. Recently he has plunged into rather serious trouble. We here at the home office under the circumstances must remove him as our representative in that particular city. In fact, we had it in mind to discharge him, but before doing so, because of his wife, we would like to give him another chance. We are unable to decide whether we are justified in giving him another opportunity. Before arriving at a final decision my associates and I are requesting you to interview this young couple and give us your reaction."

This prominent personnel man brought the young husband and wife to my office for the interview.

"Well," I asked, "what is the trouble? I am here to help you, so tell me all about it."

To which the young man replied, "I had to come to New York to see the big bosses. They wanted to see me."

"What about?" I asked.

"Well," he answered, "things weren't going so well."

"Why not?" I queried.

"I got into trouble," he replied.

"What kind of trouble?" I asked.

His wife then spoke up, "Go on and tell him."

"Well," he said, "in our business we have a great many young women. I did wrong."

I said, "With one of the girls?"

He confirmed my suspicion and continued, "They called me up here and said it had created such a scandal they would have to let me go. I brought my wife along with me. At the office they said that I was a bad influence and that I had lost my discipline in the organization. They are now deciding whether to give me another chance in a different branch in some other city. I don't know what ever made me do it, but I told them I was going outside and tell my wife. They said that was my responsibility. I went out and told her. It was a terrible experience but I told her all about it."

"How long ago did you tell her?" I asked.

He said, "A half hour ago."

"Well, what did the officers of your firm say then?"

"They sent me over to see you," he replied.

I turned to the wife, "Is there anything more you want to know?"

"Yes," she answered, "I want to know if this is the only time."

"Yes, it is the only time," he replied.

But I didn't believe him and said, "You had better tell us everything, get the whole business straightened out right now, let's get it over with. Tell us of every time. This operation has to be performed, so let's get at it."

To which he earnestly replied, "That is all. I pledge to you before God that this is the only time I have been unfaithful to my wife."

I then turned to the young woman and said, "Is there anything more you want to ask? Ask every question now because before you leave this room, I want you to promise me you will never ask him another question about it. Your mind must not dwell on this thing for your own future happiness and your future relationship with each other."

She asked a few questions and he answered them fully.

I then asked him, "Do you want to be a good man?"

He replied, "I do with all my heart."

I then asked, "Do you love this girl?"

His answer was firm. "Yes."

I then asked her, "Do you love him?"

She countered with, "I find it difficult to say yes. But down deep I do."

I then suggested that we pray. Without my instructing them to do so, they went down on their knees. I said to the husband, "You pray." He looked at me despairingly but I reiterated, "Go on, you must pray." There was a long, long silence, and then he started to pray, slowly, hesitantly, with great embarrassment and then all of a sudden with a veritable gushing out of everything that had been pent up in his mind. It was a complete purging of the soul. It moved me profoundly, but not half so much as when she started to pray. She fought with her inmost soul before my eyes; in the hearing of my ears such a battle of faith I had never heard before. That broke me up even more.

When the atmosphere cleared and they stood up before me

in one of the most primitive and basic human relationships, they looked each other straight in the eye and searched each other's eyes. It seemed to me that they stood so for minutes and that my presence was quite forgotten. Then she said to him, "If we have faith in God and in each other, we can build again."

Before they left my office I had to say to this young wife, "I have met many great people in my time, but I want to say to you, young lady, that you are one of the greatest human beings I ever met." And to the boy, I said, "You ought to thank Almighty God that He gave you such a woman as this." Her words have haunted me ever since—for it is the great answer to all such problems—"If we have faith in God and in each other, we can build again."

In this situation faith gave the wife sufficient control to hold her steady in a terrific crisis into which without warning she was plunged. It also enabled the young husband to be entirely honest with himself, a ruthless honesty which precluded any attempt at rationalization. He had done a wrong and he knew it and he said so quite frankly. His faith had provided him with a sharp perception of the exact line of demarcation between good and bad. He did not debate with himself or with his wife or with me whether he had done right or wrong. He knew. Many people who flounder in such a situation do so either because they do not know what is right or wrong or else they attempt to dispute the matter not only with others but, what is more tragic, they dispute it with themselves. Religious faith gives you a clear knowledge and understanding. You just *know* what is right and what is wrong. In the vernacular, "You don't kid yourself."

So being honest with yourself you get to the bottom of the trouble all at once. The Christian faith of these two people also helped them to believe that no matter what had happened, it could be put behind them; that having cleared the matter up, they could build again. Such people having a deep faith realize that there are no hopeless situations. He is a wise man who builds up some real faith for himself against crises which may come.

I cannot advocate too strongly that marriages be built upon spiritual foundations. One of the wisest statements ever made is that solemn assertion in the Bible, "Except the Lord build the House, they labor in vain that build it." (Psalm 127:1.) This statement is from the Book which reveals more precise knowledge about people than any other book in history. It simply states a solemn and irrevocable fact that you cannot build a successful marriage upon any other basis than the principles of love, beauty, forbearance, mutual respect and faith taught by Christianity.

It is very significant when you think about it that the old-time American families had family prayer in the home. Until recently, family prayer was one of the characteristic features of happy American home life. The divorce rate has climbed ever since people generally gave it up. This fact seems to be more than a coincidence. Marriages were consecrated in prayer. Husband and wife prayed together and had grace at the table. When the children came, it was made a family prayer period. It did something to people. It taught them how to live together and it kept them free from those mistakes which destroy marriage. Unconsciously over the years it built up character, a sturdy kind of character which molded a great free people and preserved their institutions of freedom.

Over a period of years I have found that when you can get

a couple to pray together from the very day they are married, the surest preventative to marriage difficulties has been found. I would go so far as to say that I do not know of a single couple who have practiced this who have not had happiness in marriage. It will restore married happiness to people whose marriages seem to be entering upon difficulties.

Here is a convincing illustration. A young woman came for an interview. She was quite distressed and told me that her married life was rapidly approaching the breaking point. I gathered from what she said that the fault was largely her husband's. The counselor, however, must always keep balanced, remembering there are always two sides. Finally we made her feel that perhaps she had some responsibility about the situation. Her husband, it seemed, was given to violent outbursts of temper and profanity. She pictured him as a very irritable man with whom to live. I asked if there was any religious atmosphere in the home and she acknowledged that there was none at all.

"Oh," she said, "my husband does talk a great deal about God, but not in the way you mean."

I outlined to her my theory that when a husband and wife pray together, they lift their problems above bickering into a region where quarrels fade away and where peace and understanding endure.

"Do you ever return thanks at the table in your home?" I asked.

"No," she replied, "when I was at home with my mother and father as a little girl they had grace at the table. I did learn a little prayer of grace from my father, one that he often used, but since we have been married, we have never prayed together and have never returned thanks at the table, although we are members of a church." (They never went to church except at Easter.)

"Why not begin the practice?" I asked. "When you sit down to dinner tonight, just say to your husband, 'Jim, I sort of feel I would like to return thanks. Do you mind?' Do not be strained or self-conscious or pious about it, just do it and then start talking about something else."

She seemed very doubtful and hesitant but finally agreed to apply this prescription to their matrimonial situation. Later she told me what happened. Her husband solemnly sat down to the table and glumly started to eat. She said softly, "Jim, I sort of feel like I would like to return thanks, do you mind?"

Astonishment spread over his features but he said nothing. This went on for two or three nights. He listened to his wife's voice in prayer. Perhaps he detected a tone he had not heard in a long while. One night he growled, "Who is the head of this house anyway? I am going to return thanks myself."

Presently it go so when in discussing their problems, it seemed quite natural to pray about them. The atmosphere of the home gradually changed. Bickering and argument waned and both the husband and the wife have told me that it is next to a miracle the way in which this simple practice provided the basis for happy married life.

In a certain American city a man said they had one of the most beautiful suburbs in the country. He insisted that we drive out to see it. His appraisal was correct; two or three hundred acres of the most beautifully landscaped terrain were dotted by lovely homes, each one architecturally picturesque. The residents of these homes were the leading younger married people of the city; leading, that is, from the standpoint of position and money. The man waxed enthusiastic over these houses, particularly about the fact that they contained the finest home bars that he had ever seen. It appeared that each home owner vied with his neighbor as to who could have the most attractive bar in his house.

I asked if these people were churchgoers, to which he replied with surprise, "Oh, no, very few of them go to church, except Easter maybe."

I asked if their parents had been church people.

"Oh, yes, almost without exception, the former generation were religious people."

"Well," I asked, "did their fathers and mothers have bars as nice as these bars?"

"Oh, my, no," he said, "they didn't have bars."

"That is strange," I commented. "I can't imagine any well regulated household not having a bar!"

Then I inquired as to the marriage status of these people—whether there were many divorces among them.

"Of course," he replied, "most of them have been divorced. In fact, only three or four are living with their first wife or first husband." Then he whispered surreptitiously, "There are lots of goings on around here that wouldn't look good in print."

"Pretty risqué, if you ask me," he confided.

I do not want to exaggerate but one wonders if we have arrived at the time when the family altar has given way to the family bar. In moments of sober reflection every American must ask himself what is going to happen to the country that substitutes the family bar for the family altar? Is there any relation between the break-up of the family and the entrance of liquor into the family in this dominating manner? The reader must decide this question for himself on the basis of the evidence, "Which will hold a marriage together and develop children of character—the family altar or the family bar?"

Many so-called expert solutions of marriage difficulties are offered today. Innumerable articles are written on "What is happening to marriage." Everybody is becoming intensely concerned about the breakup of the family. America was built upon certain institutions, principally the home, the church and the school. If the home collapses, what will happen to American civilization? Cicero said, "The empire is at the fireside."

Basically there is one principle for married happiness and the establishment of an enduring home and that is an atmosphere of religion in the family. Whatever your religion may be—Protestant, Catholic, or Jewish—put it into practice in your home. It is amazing how the difficulties that make for marital and family unhappiness will disappear.

A marine engineer who had been to sea for twelve years married a young widow who had one son. He had never been compelled to adjust to any family or business situation. The wife, widowed at twenty, had for ten years carried on her husband's business in a man's world. She supported herself, her son and her mother by this business. The mother lived with them in a tiny apartment and worked in the office of her daughter's business.

The young widow met the marine engineer in a service club during the war. They were quickly married but for the first six months never had more than two days together at a time, these being when he was in port. The war ended and they started life together. He began to take over the business which she owned and had operated. He moved into the already overcrowded apartment. In fact, he was moving into a new world in every way. Both the husband and the wife were high-grade people but adjustments seemed so difficult that people said, "It can't be done." The couple, too, were becoming sure that they had made a mistake. They were fed up, regretted the marriage, and were at the breaking point.

During this time they attended church regularly. They became interested in a young married couples' group at the church. One day they frankly shared their problems and defeats with another couple who from experience had learned how spiritual faith can remake and enrich marriage. This other young couple challenged them to stop the practice of constantly looking at the problems in their situation and in each other that caused or aggravated the condition and instead to start definitely asking for God's help.

They were also challenged to honestly examine themselves, to see what was wrong in their own attitudes, and to deal positively with resentments and fears. They began to replace these faults with understanding, patience and faith. They were urged to seek spiritual changes in themselves, and thus through changing themselves to change the situation.

They admitted they had tried everything but God; they had even been to a psychiatrist. The idea of God as a personal friend and positive factor in the situation, the idea that He would be concerned with the details of their lives, was entirely new to them.

They joined the other young couple in praying audibly and asked that the above change take place. They "surrendered" themselves to God's will. One week later in a small group they related that a miracle had happened and indeed their personal appearance confirmed it. They seemed to be completely released and obviously were in love in a deeper way. New confidence came to the husband which immediately affected and changed his business contacts, resulting in an amazingly fine order. New joy radiated the personality of the wife.

They began at once to practice in the home morning and evening prayer periods during which they asked for answers to the daily problems that confronted them. Both prayed audibly. They instituted the practice of a quiet period during which they said they were listening for God's guidance. They adopted the practice that when a business problem confronted them, instead of each belligerently telling the other what ought to be done, they sought jointly in prayer to find the Christian way to deal with it.

When problems arise with the teen-age boy, the wife's son, they sit down with him and all three read from the Bible, pray together and seek the best way to meet the problem. There is no longer division or jealousy in their decisions with the boy but instead an attitude of teamwork prevails, all three of them being on the "home team." This couple are so completely filled with this new spirit that they positively believe it can solve any problem. They are constantly and eagerly helping other couples who have missed domestic peace, enlightening them on the marvelous way in which it can be obtained. They are sure they have a formula which will guarantee to any husband and wife the enjoyment of married happiness.

Proceeding inductively from our clinical case histories, let me close with a few simple and practical procedures for creating a spiritual atmosphere in the home:

1. Get in the habit of saying a pleasant thing as the first words you speak in the morning. Say something of a happy and constructive nature. That will set the mental and emotional tone for the day.
2. Everybody in the home should get up five minutes earlier and utilize those extra minutes for silent

prayer—*everybody* at the table for this period. Then let one member of the family offer a few words of prayer. This serves to control the usual hectic start of the day's work.

3. Find one of the early morning religious radio programs which seems helpful. *Sit down quietly* and listen to it.

4. Say grace at lunch. If the wife is alone, let her have a quiet moment of meditation thanking God for her family and asking for guidance.

5. At dinner, say grace. Make a rule that no problems, worries or resentments shall enter into the table conversation. Make anyone who so offends drop a nickel into a bank.

6. At the close of the meal let one member of the family read a few verses of scripture. Vary this occasionally with an inspiring poem or a stimulating paragraph from a spiritual book. Let the one who prays thank God for the other members of the family by name.

7. Don't get glum when you do this. A sour expression does not denote religion. Gaiety does.

8. Take the whole family to church on Sunday and sit together in a "family pew."

9. Keep good religious literature on the home reading tables.

10. Keep a Bible on your night table and drop a few great texts into your mind before going to sleep. Psychologists say that what you think about in the last five minutes before sleep has a deep effect on your consciousness. Thank God for all the blessings of the day. Then as you turn out the light, repeat these words: "He giveth his beloved sleep." Then believe that God

is giving you deep and refreshing sleep and it will be so.

Write it above the fireplace in every home and engrave it on the mind of every husband and wife in the land—"EXCEPT THAT THE LORD BUILD THE HOUSE, THEY LABOR IN VAIN THAT BUILD IT."

Chapter Twelve

HOW TO MEET SORROW

Why should a book on success and happiness contain a chapter dealing with the technique of meeting sorrow? The obvious answer is that sorrow cannot be escaped. Sorrow is a great shock and its effect on anyone, one way or another, is profound. It may make one a bigger and finer person, or it may cloud the mind and dull the spirit. It may dissipate enthusiasm and destroy incentive. In short, one must know how to meet sorrow; how to summon courage and carry on. What can a person in sorrow get hold of that will preserve the values of his life?

The late Ernie Pyle, famous war correspondent, wrote a moving story of his walk on the beaches of Normandy late on the afternoon of D-Day. The sand was strewn with the personal effects of American boys, who early that morning had landed in a history-shaping invasion. Scattered about were touching little personal keepsakes, snapshots, books, letters. Beside the body of one boy he found a guitar, and by another a tennis racket. Touching thought—American boys going into battle, even then irrepressible tourists as in the days of peace, taking along tennis rackets and guitars.

Alongside the body of one lad, he saw half buried in the sand an issue Bible. Ernie Pyle picked up the Bible, walked a half a mile with it, then walked back and laid it down where he found it. "I don't know why I picked it up," he said, "or why I put it back down."

Perhaps he thought vaguely he would send it to the parents of the boy to comfort them. Perhaps he returned the Bible to the spot where he found it because dimly he felt that the boy having died in this faith, the Book ought to remain forever with him.

Whatever his reasons, the incident suggests that in the solemn questions of life and death, there is only one Book that has the answers that satisfy our minds and give understanding and comfort. People gain great victory over sorrow by means of their faith.

I sat with a prominent businessmen in his beautiful home. His wife was dead and he was in deep grief. About his house was all that wealth could provide of beauty and loveliness. Costly rugs were on the floor, exquisite pictures and hangings on the walls. But what did it all matter? A beloved wife was gone and a man whom I knew to be a strong leader in the business world was broken with grief.

What he told me in the intimate friendship of that hour of sorrow was impressive. He was a man of somewhat austere mien with no outward evidence of sentiment in his nature—a typical aggressive and efficient businessman of the sort that compels respect and gains dominance. Within his home, however, he was dependent, leaning upon his wife who had been almost a mother to him. He was shy about social contacts, and much preferred to remain at night quietly in his home reading, his wife knitting, or reading, at the opposite side of the table. Like many men of similar type, he was a boy never quite grown up, but putting on a strong front before the world.

"I've found something in religion that I never felt before," he said quietly. "Last night I knelt by my bed as usual to pray. I've done this every night since I was a boy. When I was married forty years ago," he continued, "my wife and I agreed to pray together every night. We would kneel by the side of the bed and she would pray out loud. I couldn't do that," he explained, " and anyway she was much better at it and I always felt God would listen to her."

Rather shyly he said that he would hold his wife's hand as she prayed. Like two simple-hearted children they were. God must have looked with delight upon them, judging from the way he blessed them.

"Well," he went on, "we did that all these years and then—then God took her away, and last night I knelt alone. Out of long habit I put my hand out for hers, but it was not there. It all came over me then how I missed her and loved her, and I wanted her so badly I could hardly bear it. I felt as I did long ago when I was a boy and was scared and wanted my mother. I put my head down on the bedside and I guess for the first time in my life I really prayed. I said, 'O God, I've heard about people really finding you and I believe you do help people. You know how much I need you. I put my life in your hands. Help me, dear Lord.' "

He looked me full in the face, and his eyes were filled with wonder as he said, "Do you know what happened? His words came slowly. "Suddenly I felt a touch on my hand, the hand she always held. It was a strong, kindly touch, and I seemed to feel a great hand take my own. In surprise I looked up, but, of course, could see no one. However all the pain seemed to go out of my mind and peace came into my heart. I knew that God was with me and would never leave me, and that she is with me too." So he concluded with determination in his voice.

This man had discovered a basic fact taught by Christianity; that fact is that *what seems to be death is not death at all*. Apparently Jesus Christ did not think of death as we think of it. As he stood by the body of a little girl, he said, "Weep not; she is not dead, but sleepeth." When He came to the bereaved household of Lazarus, He informed them, "Our friend Lazarus sleepeth; but I go, that I may awake him out of sleep." It would seem that death to Him is a condition of sleep. In His teaching actual death is something more sinister than physical death. He teaches that the body is only a temporary house for an eternal soul. Apparently death in the mind of Jesus Christ means death of the soul. He said, "The soul that sinneth, it shall die." "The wages of sin is death" (i.e., for the soul). Historically as civilizations become pagan they tend to increase emphasis upon the body as the ultimate value. The teaching of Christianity, however, is "Be not afraid of them that kill the body."

In His thought, what we call death does not in any sense affect the continuity of the individual's life. The New Testament contains a magnificent passage which describes the state of our deceased loved ones; "They shall hunger no more, neither thirst any more; neither shall the sun light on them, nor any heat. For the Lamb which is in the midst of the throne shall feed them, and shall lead them unto living fountains of waters: and God shall wipe away all tears from their eyes." (Revelation 7:16-17.)

That is one of the most comforting passages ever written. They shall hunger no more. What hunger? Hunger of the body? Mental or spiritual hunger? Whatever it is, they shall hunger no more, but will be satisfied. Nor shall they thirst any more. Perhaps thirst is a more poignant description than hunger for it is a deeper anguish when experienced. The point is that our loved ones have their deepest longings and yearnings completely satisfied.

The passage also indicates that their life shall be so full and beautiful that it can only be described by the loveliness of fountains of living waters. And "every tear shall be wiped away from their eyes."

After my mother's death, as I relived our life together, I remembered one lovely Sunday afternoon when together we saw the famous fountains of Versailles. Like myriads of diamonds in the sunlight, the fountains played to the delight of my mother.

She was a very great traveler and visited many countries. She was, in truth, a connoisseur of beauty. One rainy night she fell into ecstasy as she contemplated a ferry boat running between Manhattan and Hoboken. She commented in ecstatic tones on its romance and charm, on the mystery of the river, the night and the rain and the boat with its lights in the mist.

After she passed away it gave me comfort to think of her as being taken by God's hand and hearing him say, "Come unto me, I will show you more marvelous fountains than those you once saw at Versailles." I am sure that she eagerly followed. I can almost see the dancing fountains reflected in her eyes. It is not difficult to think of God as wiping tears from her eyes. As she loved to travel and used to write enthusiastically that she was having a glorious time and only wished we could be with her, so I believe that though she is out of sight at present, she is having a time of great happiness. It would not be fair to her to want her back from that land of ineffable charm. I can imagine her making mental notes of places of beauty and she probably says to herself. "When my husband and children come here, won't it be a delight to show them these beautiful places which I have found and enjoyed?"

A veteran nurse says: "It has always seemed to me a major tragedy that so many people go through life haunted by the fear of death—only to find when it comes that it's as natural as life itself. For very few are afraid to die when they get to the very end. In all my experience only one seemed to feel any terror—a woman who had done her sister a wrong which it was too late to right.

"Something strange and beautiful happens to men and women when they come to the end of the road. All fear, all horror disappears. I have often watched a look of happy wonder dawn in their eyes when they realized this was true. It is all part of the goodness of nature and, I believe, of the illimitable goodness of God."*

Do not hold on to your loved ones in your thought. Release them, let them go. You do not lose them by so doing. You hamper them with your dark and dismal thoughts of grief. They have earned the joy and delight which they are now experiencing. Do not spoil it for them.

I visited a little old-fashioned country burying ground one winter day with a friend. This man had met with outstanding success but he told me that when his mother died he felt that life was not worth living. He did not marry until late in life and had spent his earlier years in great devotion to his mother. His happiest experiences did not consist in the attainment of some sought-after ambition, but were the pleasure of going home and telling his mother about them. When she died, and this was no longer possible, he said that

---

Getting the Most Out of Life, an Anthology from *The Reader's Digest*, p. 116.

life seemed to lose its meaning. There was nothing to work for any more. He was somewhat bitter and found himself constantly seeking his mother out in his thoughts and resisting the idea that she had passed from him.

As we stood in this little burying ground, he said, "That is the way I felt until one day I came to this place." He had shown me a little crossroad store that had been operated by his father, and after the father's death, by his mother. "She was a frail little woman," he said, "but her sparkling black eyes never showed any defeat. She had little education and few opportunities. She had to work hard to bring up her little family. As a small boy I saw her drag heavy bags of sugar across the floor of the store. She would pull and I would get behind and push.

"Then came the night before I went away to college. She took me into her room and, reaching under the mattress, pulled out four crumpled ten dollar bills. 'I have saved them for you,' she said. 'Take them, go to college, work hard and become a fine, outstanding man.' "

He said, "I shall never forget those crumpled bills resting in her little hands. I noted how worn her hands were and it touched my heart.

"So, when she died, I did not want to live. But one day I stood in this cemetery and looked at the old familiar hills capped with snow. It was all very peaceful and the stark beauty of the world in the cold winter sunshine gave me a sense of eternity. I prayed, using the same words that she used to use. All at once I had a peculiar feeling of peace and inner quietness. A thought came that had never previously occurred to me. It was that I was not being fair to my mother. She had worked hard and now for the first time she was free of labor and toil.

"All her life she had read about heaven. I could still hear her voice singing, 'There is a land of pure delight.' She was one of those simple Christians for whom earth was a preparation for heaven, and I was not allowing her to enjoy this heaven for which she had labored and toiled, and of which she had dreamed. So, standing in that little cemetery I spoke out loud, 'Mother, I am going to let you go, have a good time, you have earned this joy.' As soon as I said that, I had peace in my heart. It was as if she actually came and stood beside me and said, "Thank you, my son, you understand. I will wait for you and meet you across the river. Meanwhile my spirit will often be near you.' "

There is a natural wistfulness regarding the state and condition of our loved ones, when they have passed from this life. We have no exact information but there is sufficient reason to believe that our loved ones who died in the faith are in the kindly hands of God.

It must be a beautiful place to which they have gone. We know *nothing* about it, of course, but we do have intimations. When that great wizard of the natural sciences, Thomas A. Edison, came to die, it was noticed that he was attempting to give a message. His physician, bending low, heard Mr. Edison say faintly but distinctly, "It is very beautiful over there."

A minister told of being with a dying man. The family gathered in his room felt it must be dark going through the valley all alone, so they lighted all the lights that the dying man would not be afraid of going into the dark. Of a sudden at midnight he raised his head on the pillow, and with a look of surprise said, "Put out the lights. Can't you see, the sun is up."

I knew the meterologist in a certain city. He had held his

position for forty years. For four decades he had charted the weather and had studied natural laws. He was by instinct, training and experience, a rational and a scientific mind. He was also a man of deep religious faith. His son was not a religious person in a formal sense. When the father came to die, he suddenly turned to his son, who sat by his bedside, and said, "Bill, I see the most beautiful place. It is beyond description and...in a window is a light for me." An expression of great peace and happiness came over his face and he said no more.

When the son related this incident, I asked him, "What do you think your father actually saw?" His reply was characteristic of the scientific attitude of both father and son. "What do I think my father actually saw? Why, there is no doubt about that. He never reported anything he did not see or test or know. He saw what he said he saw."

"Could it have been an hallucination?" I asked.

"Not at all," he replied. "My father had not the type of mind to have an hallucination. He saw something and reported it precisely as was his custom with all data," said the son. "I am absolutely sure of it."

We must seek our information about the after-life from the only source that is thoroughly reliable, one that has stood the test of time. To the question, "What is the state of our loved ones after this life?", the Bible suggests the answer: "Blessed are the dead which die in the Lord." That means, "Happy are the dead who die in the Lord."

It is difficult to associate happiness with death. Death for us is the ultimate tragedy. But can anything in God's plan be a tragedy? Tennyson said, "Death is the bright side of life." Robert Louis Stevenson, when death came to him, said, "If this is death, it is easier than life." One wonders in the light of such statements and certain experiences whether death is the tragedy we think it is. We cannot believe that God, in transferring a man from one form of life to another, would make of it a tragedy.

A news reporter had to undergo a serious operation. As it was performed under local anesthesia, he had all his faculties about him, and was able to note and record his experiences. He decided he would go into this experience as a reporter, describing each step. If he came back from the edge of death, he would have a great story to tell. He found himself sinking. He came to a point where he did not want to come back. The pull was to go on. It was such an entrancing aspect of peace and beauty that every element in his nature urged him forward. It was reported afterwards by the doctor that he had a sinking spell. Then, by an act of will, he said, "I must return, I must fight off this allurement." With great reluctance he returned to normal life again, but said he would never again have a fear of death.

The process of birth holds some suggestions of the protection we may experience at the end of earthly life. An infant, snuggled up under the mother's heart in the pre-natal days, is surrounded by warmth and protection. If he could reason, the baby might say, "I don't want to be born; I don't want to go out of this world into that other world. I am happy here; I am afraid of birth."

In his pre-natal existence, he might regard birth as we do death, as the end of one certain experience and the beginning of another uncertain one. Then he is born. Looking down at him is the kindest and sweetest face in the world. He is cuddled in his mother's loving arms. There he is held and protected, fed and loved. God made it that way.

So after many years, when a man comes to die, need he be terrified at the prospect or death—or, if you please, of another birth? Should he fear to pass from this world into the next? If he had love and protection when first he came to this earth, may he not assume he will have the same as he enters the next life? Can we not trust the same God to take care of us in death as He did in birth? Will His attribute of love so quickly change? It would not be like Him.

We should learn to think of death as a natural part of our total experience. Let me relate the story of a woman who deeply understood this truth. She was past middle age when she came to see me. "I have a hard problem for you," she said. "Three of the best physicians in New York have told me that I must undergo a serious operation not later than Monday morning, and that this operation may mean my death. The doctors told me frankly, because I asked them for the truth."

She had the quality of personality that could take the truth, no matter how grim. "About a year ago," she continued, "I lost my son in the war." She showed me his picture, then said, "I ask you, sir, if I die as a result of this operation on Monday, will I see him again?"

She looked me squarely in the eye, searching intently for any indefiniteness or evasiveness. I looked directly into her eyes and told her: "It is my positive belief, based upon what I know of Jesus Christ, that you will see him again."

"How soon will that be after I go?" she asked.

"I wish I could say," I replied, "but if your son were in a foreign country and you went to see him, you would make for him as soon as the ship landed, wouldn't you? You will find him. It can't be long, for love can never lose its own."

She said, "I have a husband and a daughter. If I live, I will be with them. If I die, I shall see my son."

I said, "Yes, you are in a very fortunate position. Regardless of what happens, you still have all your family."

"God is very good," she said slowly.

When she stood up to leave, I took her by the hand and could not help saying, "You are one of the greatest personalities I ever met."

Quietly, rationally, simple, she was getting ready for a journey. When she left me, she went to a photographer and had her picture taken. Later I saw those photographs and there was a light on her face. Next, she saw her lawyer and even made arrangements for her funeral. Then, quickly and in complete peace, she went to the hospital, where she submitted to the operation. Despite the best skill of modern science, she passed on. Today, I believe, she is with both her son and her loved ones.

I cannot prove this. Long ago I got over the idea that you have to prove everything. The man who disagrees cannot disprove it. Although perhaps as yet the superiority of faith cannot be proven scientifically, yet we may reasonably consider our faith as a logic which goes beyond so-called scientific knowledge. It is the deep logic of human intuition which, in the final analysis, is an ultimate source of truth. What we feel inwardly in the logic of experience, in the flash of intuition, is true especially when millions of human beings in every generation so think and so "feel."

We live in a generation during which death has visited households as never before. Only recently death's sinister touch was on battlefields all over the globe. Death lurked beneath the sea and hid behind every white cloud. His message daily came through the mail into thousands of homes. His solemn voice came over the telegraph wires, in the form of a little yellow envelope containing a message which said, "The United States Government regrets to inform you that your son..." Then there was the shutting of a door, a stifled sob, and many an American family repeated an experience known throughout the history of our country. Death ruled the world. Even in days of peace, death is always present.

But remember this—death never wins. Write across the skies, blazon abroad that every man may hear the great and abiding faith which rises above the roar of battle, above the smoke and tumult of pain and suffering, above death itself as expressed in the lilting victorious words which have survived the centuries: "I am the resurrection, and the life: he that believeth in me, though he were dead, yet shall he live."

That is the fact we need to know: life wins an everlasting and glorious victory over death.

During the late war the chaplains went with the troops to the very front. This accounts for the high casualty rate among chaplains. Catholic, Protestant, Jewish chaplains, they were in danger with the boys.

When a boy lay wounded or dying on the field, perhaps the first man to bend over him was the chaplain. The Christian chaplain wore on his helmet a little white cross—the Cross of Christ. The first thing that the eyes of the wounded man would see was the white cross on the helmet just above him. One thinks of a boy struck down, feeling death approach. Perhaps a terror wells up within that he wouldn't admit to anybody. A wave of homesickness and loneliness comes over him. He would give anything to see the face of his mother, or his wife, or the face of his sweetheart, or feel the touch of the hands of his little children. He would like once again to see the sunlight falling on the old hills of his native land. He would like to see the sparkle of the Hudson, the Ohio, or the Mississippi, but that is all very, very far away, except that it is printed in his heart. He is dying far from home and loved ones.

A kindly face bends over him. He sees on the helmet the cross and something responds in his heart. The Church is here. The faith has followed him. The tie that binds still holds and the everlasting arms are beneath him. Then the chaplain, out of the kindness of his heart, puts his hand under the head of the dying boy, perhaps strokes back his hair just as his mother would have done, and says, "Son, listen, you remember these words, don't you, boy? Believe them. Believe them with all your heart: 'I am the resurrection, and the life: he that believeth in me, though he were dead, yet shall he live.' "

The boy listens, peace comes into his heart. His eyes grow hazy. Earth recedes; the face grows dim, the voice fades. For just a moment he is crossing a valley. And then almost more quickly than it takes to tell it, suddenly everything is bright around him and there is a glorious light and a radiance more wonderful than anything he has ever seen or known.

He looks up in happy surprise. There is a face above him, but it is another face, stronger, more kindly, even than the other face that he saw through his pain. Again he sees a cross, but this time it is shining in light and he hears words like rippling music, tender words, words of triumph and faith and the voice that utters them is the voice that formulated them long ages ago, "I am the resurrection, and the life." The voice says to him, "You have found it, my boy, you have found it. I am with you as I said I would be. That man over on the earthly side of the river was my representative and he pointed you the way to cross over. You are here now with me and all is well."

It is not unreasonable to believe that in this universe, which is both material and spiritual, our loved ones who have gone from us are not really very far from us.

Many people report that when least expected they have had a definite feeling of the near presence of loved ones.

A man whose rationality I respect told me that for the first three weeks after his father's death, he suffered profound grief. "But," he said, "one day all of a sudden that grief lifted. I had a very serious problem to solve, and I almost felt that my father was there helping me to solve it. I got the touch of his mind. I felt his presence. I could not be grief-stricken longer, for it unmistakeably came over me that he was near to me."

He asked if I felt he could believe that experience to be real, and I told him that I thought so.

I have found some help in an illustration used by Steward Edward White in his book, *The Unobstructed Universe*. When the electric fan is in motion at high speed, it is possible to see through the thick blades. Mr. White makes the point that ours is an unobstructed universe, meaning that those who have passed into the spiritual world are merely living in an area of higher frequency, or a different frequency than that in which we dwell. They are near to us but we cannot see them. Man has a psychic nature governed by the laws of the spiritual universe. Thus intuitions, insights, spiritual apprehensions are not unnatural or bizarre, but are normal experiences. They are flash-overs from the spiritual world which is correlated to our own. Why they come, we do not know, but it is very dangerous to assert dogmatically that they are not real. The most likely fact is that they represent a fundamental reality in our universe, namely the indestructibility of the spirit and the deathlessness of the human soul.

I should like to conclude this chapter by relating an experience with a brokenhearted Gold Star mother. Shortly after the close of the war *The American Magazine* published a pathetic letter written by Mrs. Frank C. Douglas of Blytheville, Arkansas, in which she told how her son's death in battle had shaken her faith. I was so moved by her letter the I immediately wrote an answer, not only to her, but to all mothers everywhere who had known this crushing experience.

The American Magazine has given permission to insert here my answer to Mrs. Douglas, which it published in the issue of April, 1946. My letter was preceded by an editorial note.

In recent issue of *The American Magazine*, Mrs. Frank C. Douglas of Blytheville, Ark., told how her son's death in battle had shattered her faith in the power of prayer. Since the publication of her letter, more than 3,000 readers from all over the nation have written to offer her advice and comfort. From all these letters Mrs. Douglas selected several which she found to be especially helpful. Among them is the following letter from Dr. Norman Vincent Peale, minister of the Marble Collegiate Church of New York, noted writer and radio speaker. Dr. Peale's letter is published here in the hope that it will also be of help to others.

Dear Mrs. Douglas:

If we could always keep our loved ones alive through the exercising of faith, there would never be any death. There has to come a time when, after God has spared them time and time again, He cannot spare them longer. It is given to all men to die. Some die in youth. Others die in old age. Some die in time of peace as a result of accident or disease;

others die in time of war. I think one must assume that whenever a man dies, his life's work has been accomplished on this earth. In the thought of God, years as we measure them are as flashing seconds to Him. It makes no difference whether a man lives twenty years or eighty years, when he has finished his work here he is promoted to that higher realm of the spirit which we call heaven.

Really, it is a high honor that some men can finish their life's work at an early age, while others in the sight of God apparently do not do so well, and they have to stay here longer until they finally work it out.

It is a fact that we poor human beings think so deeply in earthly terms. God does not place the same valuation upon earthly existence that we do. He said, "Be not afraid of them who kill the body, but rather those who may destroy the soul."

Of course, this is little comfort to one who looks and longs for a beloved face and figure. But if we are thinking spiritually rather than in an earthly way, we do not lay so much importance upon the life of the body.

You have been a woman of faith. You say your son had faith. This meant that you were both in the will of God. You were harmonized with His will and purpose. I would think, then, that you ought to assume, which I am sure you may, that your son being yielded to God, His will was done.

God in His answers to prayer often says "Yes." Sometimes He says "Wait." Often he says "No." In any case, His will is done, and true faith is to believe that what has happened has happened for the best. If one does not take that attitude, he is setting his personal desire against the wisdom of God. Oftentimes we confuse with faith merely that which we desire.

I should like to ask you, in the deepest possible kindness, do you really think you have lost your son? Let me tell you a little story.

Recently I sat in the home of two good friends whose son had died in France. Two photographs were on their library wall. One was of the father in the uniform of World War I; the other was of the 20-year-old son in the uniform of this war.

In the intimacy of friendship they talked tenderly of their son. "He always whistled," the mother said. "Far down the street, when he came home from school as a little boy, you could hear him whistling, and as he grew up he whistled. He would come dashing into the house whistling, and toss his coat and hat at the hall hatrack; and both would catch the peg and hang there. Then he would run up the stairs whistling. He was a gay spirit."

They told humorous incidents; and, in that intimate way of friendship, we were laughing—and occasionally the laughter would be through tears. Suddenly, the mother said sadly, "But we will never hear him whistle again."

Strange as it seems, at that moment I had an indistinct, but nevertheless real, feeling that I had "heard" the boy whistle as we talked. It might have been the mood we were in, yet I prefer to believe differently; but as she said, "We will never hear him whistle again," I found myself saying, "You are wrong about that"—I hesitated—"I had a feeling that right this minute he was whistling in this room."

The father—a sturdy, unemotional person—spoke up quickly: "Strange that you should say that: I had the same feeling myself." We sat hushed and awed. Ingersoll's great line passed through my mind—"In the night of death, hope sees a star, and listening love can hear the rustle of a wing."

In the faith that God will give you peace and understanding, I am—Cordially yours—Norman Vincent Peale.

Chapter Thirteen

CHANGE YOUR THOUGHTS AND YOU CHANGE EVERYTHING

Change your thoughts and everything changes. Your life is determined by the kind of thoughts you habitually think.

If, however, your thoughts do not change, you will follow your old life pattern as the following story shows...

A hotel manager told me that a Barbers' Supply Association held a convention in his hotel. This organization had a very enterprising publicity agent. He went down to a poor street in a bad section and found the most unpromising specimen of human nature he could locate—an unkempt, unshaven, drunken, sad creature. This down-and-outer was taken to the hotel where they gave him a haircut; dressed him in a good suit of clothes; gave him nice linen. They decked him out in a rakish looking overcoat and cane and spats. When he emerged from this refurbishing, he was a marvelous example of the barber's art. Meanwhile, they had photographed every process of this transformation, and each photograph appeared in the daily newspaper. It was hailed as a first-rate publicity stunt. Everybody was amazed at what the barbers could do, with the help of the tailors, in making over a man. The hotel manager was impressed. After the convention his interest in the man remained.

He said to him, "By a strange set of circumstances you

have been made into the form of a gentleman, and lifted out of the slums. Now your great opportunity is at hand. I am going to give you a job in another hotel which I operate, and I am going to back you, and we are going to make a successful man of you. When will you go to work?"

The man replied, "Suppose we make it tomorrow morning at eight o'clock."

A doubt crossed the mind of the hotel manager, but he agreed. The doubt came back at eight o'clock next morning when his man did not show up. Nor did he appear all day. So the manager, following a hunch, went down to the same street from which the man had come and after a search found him dead drunk, sleeping on some newspapers in an alley, his fine clothes rumpled and soiled.

The hotel manager said that it was a most disillusioning experience. "The barbers may be able to clean him up on the outside, but you can never make anything out of a man until you also change him on the inside," and he added ruefully, "I wish I could have had him just a little longer, for the thing that was wrong with that man was his thought processes. Maybe if I could have had him a little longer, I could have changed his thinking and so have changed him."

To make amends for his depressing story, the hotel manager told me another.

"I have somebody to counteract the man who reverted to his old thoughts," he said. "It is Jimmy, the elevator boy and bellhop. He was sent to me by a church school for delinquent boys. He was a bright lad, greeted everybody politely, was always courteous. He worked hard and had good moral habits. One day the boy came to me and said, 'I am going to get married. Will you be the best man?' " So this big hotel manager was best man for a bellhop, which was just like him.

He became interested in the boy and one day said to him, "Jimmy, you are an unusual fellow. What makes you this way? You have something that is missing in a good many boys. What is that something?"

Jimmy answered, "Oh, I don't know unless it is what they did for us down at the school."

"Well," he asked, "what did they do for you at the school?"

The boy replied thoughtfully, "Oh, I don't know unless it is that they got us to thinking—kinda religious—I guess that's it. They got us to thinking kinda religious."

Of course Jimmy has gone ahead. He discovered that life is what your thoughts make it. He learned to think "kinda religious."

A man's world is not primarily made of the circumstances that surround him. The kind of thoughts he thinks determines the exact kind of world in which he lives. You are not what you think you are, but what you *think*, you are.

The wisest men of all time have said this. Nineteen hundred years ago there lived a Roman Emperor by the name of Marcus Aurelius. He has been called the wisest man of the Roman Empire. On his long marches and military campaigns, he sat by his campfire writing his thoughts. These thoughts were gathered together in a book called *The Meditations of Marcus Aurelius*, one of the greatest heritages from antiquity. And one of the greatest things that this wise man said is this: "Your life is what your thoughts make of it."

The wisest man who ever lived in the United States of America, some people say, was Ralph Waldo Emerson. And he said, "A man is what he thinks about all day long."

And the wisest of all Books declares, "As a man thinketh

in his heart (i.e., as a man thinketh in his subconscious mind), so is he."

What you think, what you have been thinking over a long period of time, what you are going to think in the days ahead will determine precisely what you are and the kind of world you live in. What you think determines what you become.

Change your thoughts and you will change the world. Change your thoughts correctly and everything will change into inner peace, happiness and personal power.

"Be ye transformed by the renewing of your mind." (Romans 12:2) No wiser thing was ever said. You can transform yourself, the world in which you live, your home conditions, your business conditions, in fact your whole life, by a spiritual renewing of your thoughts.

This book advocates a formula of living that assigns large importance to the power of our thoughts in changing the conditions of our lives. The secret, as Jimmy, the bellhop, said, is to think "kinda religious." Normal spiritual thinking can so change a person's life as to make everything different.

Thought patterns which have been traced over a long period of time are difficult to modify. Wrong thinking becomes habit and habitual procedures resist change. Fortunately in Christianity we have a phenomenon called "spiritual experience." It is a process by which God's power accomplishes in our minds, sometimes instantly, what laborious, tedious, correction would require months to achieve. This is not to say that all spiritual experience is instantaneous. Often, indeed more often, it is a process of growth and progressive development. In whatever way spiritual experience occurs, it is a method superior to psychological discipline and is more effective and certain of permanence. This comparison is not to be interpreted as minimizing the value of psychological discipline, a value I readily grant.

Condition your mind to spiritual change by practicing spiritual thinking. Read the Bible regularly. Commit its passages to memory, thus constantly feeding your mind material which will remake its attitudes. Know spiritually minded people and experience the gradual mental change which results from spiritual conversation. Subject your mind to the atmosphere in which spiritual experience occurs; go to church regularly. Get your mind into the habit of prayer. Think about God and Christ at every opportunity. Persevere until you find yourself enjoying this plan of disciplining your thinking. In this process you are changing your thought pattern, making it possible for spiritual experience to change everything for you.

The great change may come when least expected. I was in a certain city one day and between engagements went into a large downtown bookstore. The head sales person was a very pleasant little elderly lady. We got into conversation and she told me she had been in that store for a great many years.

"I would like to ask you a question," I said. "What type of book has the greatest sale today?"

"Oh," she said, "the answer to that is easy. It is books dealing with self-improvement and books dealing with religion." Then she volunteered the opinion that the highest form of self-improvement is religious writings.

Naturally I was interested to know that the general public was buying this type of literature, and then she commented, "The most unlikely type of people seem to be buying religious reading. They aren't what you would call saintly people but they are young folk, every-day people, all kinds, business people and for the most part men. Would you like to hear of an interesting incident that happened here recently?" she asked.

Assured of my interest she said, "One day not long ago a tall, lanky soldier came into the store. He was over six feet and as thin as a rail. Yet he was whistling exuberantly, with total unconcern for the presence of others; just whistling out of a heart that was obviously overflowing with joy. 'My, my.' I exclaimed, 'somebody is certainly happy.' He gave a broad grin and replied, 'I sure am, ma'am, I sure am happy. I have just come back from overseas. I was in a German prison for a long time and I lost forty pounds.'

" 'I don't see anything in that to make you so happy.' I said.

" 'Oh,' he said, 'you don't understand, so I will tell you.'

" 'In that prison we had very little to read. Anything in print that came our way was devoured by the boys. One day there came into my hands an old, worn, dog-eared copy of a religious novel that was widely read a few years back.'

"He said, 'Back in the United States I never would have looked at this book. I never went to church or anything, for I always had the idea that churches were dull, stuffy places, and they never would get me inside of one, except maybe on Easter.'

"This book was the story of how everybody who came under the influence of Jesus Christ had wonderful things happen to them.

" 'Well,' he said, 'ma'am, I read that book and all of a sudden something wonderful happened to *me*. I believe Jesus Christ is alive now just the same as He was in the Bible story times, for as I read this book, I am sure He touched me. Suddenly quicker than I can tell you about, I felt happy inside of my heart and everything changed. The whole world became different. Why,' he said, 'I was set free before the American Army came. I was set free from myself, which was the greatest prison I was ever in.

" 'So,' he continued, 'I finally got back home and was reunited with my wife and she is a wonderful girl, the prettiest and sweetest there ever was, but'—he hesitated—'she is lacking something. She is heavyhearted and dull. In her mind she is pessimistic and negative. Life for her is just a hard dragging kind of thing. She is not happy. So, ma'am, I have come down to this store to get a copy of that book and I am going to read it to her in the hope that she will get what I got. I want the same thing to happen to her that happened to me.' "

What *had* happened to him? That a tremendous change had taken place in him is obvious. At the precise moment when his emotional and mental attitudes were favorable, a book able to vitally affect his thoughts came into his hands. So a spiritual experience took place and everything changed.

Other people arrive at a similar condition more gradually. They definitely set out to practice new habits and attitudes. They systematically seek help from religion and presently they, too, become aware of change in outlook, in personal relations, and in the strength and power which is theirs. It is manifested in their daily lives. Happiness comes and also a grip and mastery over circumstances.

They say of a man who knows where he is going and how to get there that he is "on the beam." This means he has reduced the element of error and is closely approximating the center of truth or efficiency.

Another common statement is, "He has something on the ball," meaning he has the skill. He has the slight extra turn. He knows how to do it.

Another such statement is, "He is in the groove," meaning he is going right straight down the center to the mark. He has mastered the matter. All of this may seem quite remote from religion, but it isn't. The Bible is very wise. It says, "Seek ye first the Kingdom of God, and his righteousness; and all things shall be added unto you." What does that mean? Simply, seek skills in God's way of doing things. Seek God's *rightness* (the word righteousness indicates "rightness," skill, genius, the slight hair's turn that makes everything different). Seek the rightness which God teaches you and you will have the skillful touch. Therefore, where you have failed heretofore, you will now acquire skill.

The pity is that a lot of people go through life blundering, failing, struggling along, never quite obtaining or achieving, when all can be different if they will learn and practice the simple principles of Christianity. Then things instead of being subtracted from them will be added unto them. Instead of life slipping from their grasp, life will flow toward them. Nothing can break them down, nothing can overwhelm them, nothing can destroy the peace, happiness and usefulness of their lives.

Another factor in the process by which changing your thoughts changes everything is the practice of the psychology of joy. If one expects to live a happy life, he must first practice thinking happy thoughts. If, as has been stated by wise men, our life is what our thoughts make of it, then it follows naturally that a joyful existence is predicted upon joyful thinking.

It is not likely that aimless thinking or the occasional and vagrant joyful thought will produce this effect. One must deliberately set about thinking happy thoughts as the normal slant of his mind. Discipline yourself daily to the practice of thinking thoughts of joy instead of succumbing to gloomy and depressed thoughts.

People manufacture their own unhappiness by the kind of thoughts they think. They may possess every factor which conceivably makes for happiness but miss a pleasant and useful existence because their thoughts have fallen into habitual gloominess or negativism. People easily develop the habit of thinking negatively. They form a thought pattern of depression and failure. As a result they feel mentally, emotionally and physically depressed.

Instead of practicing the psychology of joy, people who fail practice the psychology of pessimism. Their minds become filled with shadows and as a result life generally is full of shadows. Remember this important truth about your life—there is a definite tendency in human nature to become what you habitually think and practice. Set yourself, therefore, deliberately to be a joyful personality in your thinking. Obviously this will require practice. It will be very difficult at first as it always is when you try to overcome old mental habits. Everything in the mind resists the abandonment of a mental habit. But if you persevere and take your mind by the scruff of the neck, if one may use such a figure, tyrannizing over it, determining to control it, you will finally accomplish your purpose and your mind will yield to your new determination.

When Jesus Christ said, "These things have I spoken unto you, that my joy might remain in you, and that your joy might be full," He was stating a truth so potent, so electric, so profound that the man who ignores it misses the greatest aid to success and happiness. This truth can absolutely free a human personality. Psychologically we know that joy is a freeing and releasing agent in the mind. Joy can even make you feel better physically. It can help unlock your muscles. It can release energy. In short, it has the power to make you efficient, to get your whole personality, body, mind and spirit coordinated. Joy helps you to function efficiently. If the psychological effect of joy were better understood, it would be deliberately and enthusiastically practiced by every intelligent person.

William H. ("Little Bill") Miller,* one of our great athletic coaches, says that one of the best ways to become an athlete is to develop the psychology of joy. He was teaching a man to play golf. According to Coach Miller, the most important factor in golf is relaxation, the complete ease and freedom of muscular coordination, the absence of tension. And one way to get that, he insists, is to develop an inner spirit of joy.

Miller was once having trouble in teaching a man because the pupil was very tense and tied-up. To counteract tension, the coach said, "Joe, before you make your next shot, imagine that somebody has just told you the most uproarious joke you ever heard. Laugh heartily; then before you finish the laugh, turn around, give no thought to the technique, just swing your club, strike the ball. Have no concern about where it goes, just laugh and hit it." The man did so and the ball sailed straight as an arrow down the fairway. The coach explained, "The joy welling up within him set Joe's mind free." When the tension dropped out of Joe's mind, it dropped out of his muscles. His whole being became coordinated through the therapeutic of joy. He became a unified

---

*Author of *How to Relax* (Scientific Body Control).

personality and the stroke was natural with the result that it was good.

On another occasion Miller was teaching a girl to play tennis. Her techniques were correct, but still she was not a successful player. The coach said, "Let's sing as we play."

Rather self-consciously she started to sing. But when she got into the rhythm of the song, strangely enough she discovered it was the rhythm of the game. She forgot herself, lost herself. Her strokes fell into natural form and she struck the ball properly as she sang. She became released, and being filled with joy played excellently.

Learn the skill of living. Practice your religion. Think joy, not gloom.

One marvels at the astute wisdom of Jesus. Today the great scientific thinkers of our time are only beginning to learn principles which He taught two thousand years ago. Think of it, twenty centuries ago He told us that the psychology of joy releases people. Now in this modern age psychiatrists, athletic coaches, students of the human mind, are just beginning to recognize the truth of these teachings. He was the first to instruct us that when a person feels his thoughts with spiritual joy, it sets free creative abilities and makes for happiness and success.

This thing called spiritual experience plus the practicing of the simple techiques of the Christian faith produces the thought changes which make for happiness and successful living.

Let me call as witnesses several types of people who have experienced the change of thought and life outlined above.

At a dinner party, I sat beside a famous actress. Two other ministers sat at our end of the table. One of these ministers was an elderly man and had been one of the most eminent clergymen in the United States. The other minister is known round the world, a great and eloquent orator. The older minister is the best story teller I have ever heard, bar none. Had he gone on the stage, he would certainly have been a famous comedian.

The second man was also a capital story teller. I chimed in with my own poor little stories. One story after another by three ministers—a sort of ministerial "Can You Top This?"—kept the party in an uproar. Had there been a "laugh meter," it would have registered high scores.

Finally the famous actress shook her head in wonderment and said, "I never heard anything like it. I have been in all kinds of parties, and in the most sophisticated night spots, but I never met three such gay lads as you ministers."

She looked sharply at us and asked, "You haven't had anything have you? Personally I can't get that happy until I have had several."

I started to say, "Of course not," when the elderly minister intercepted me and replied, "Yes, we have had something. Yes, madam, we are intoxicated."

His face was so radiant and his eyes so alight that she understood and said softly, "I know what you mean." She understood that Christ so completely releases people from dwarfing, crippling thoughts and emotions that life never grows stale.

Some years ago I spoke to several hundred young people at a convention. They were a gay and happy crowd, a rakish looking lot too. Judging by their outlandish attire, I thought, "This is certainly a sophisticated crowd." I found that I was right; they were sophisticated. Sophistication means worldly wise. Supposedly, a sophisticated person is one who knows what it is all about, and how to get happiness out of life. He knows his way around. On the other hand, certain bored, cynical pagans you see yawning around are not truly sophisticated. They are not worldly wise, because they have missed happiness. A truly sophisticated person is one who is smart enough to find out how really to be happy. Therefore, although some may be surprised to hear it, a sophisticated person is a spiritual person.

I never encountered such an eager audience as this group of young sophisticates. They anticipated ideas before they were half uttered and at anything humorous, before you made your point, they were ahead of you and roaring with laughter. They were alert, vibrant, a crowd of the most released people I have met.

One of these boys later said in his slangy jargon, "I used to run with a pretty fast crowd but I never began to enjoy life until I got in with this gang," indicating the crowd by a wave of his hand. Then he shook his head and said, "That bunch I used to go with was a bunch of saps—honestly! I only wish I could make them understand how to really get a kick out of life."

"How *do* you get a kick out of life?" I asked.

He looked at me and, absolutely without embarrassment, replied, "Why, get Christ into your heart, that's the way to get a kick out of life."

Usually when people start talking about religion they get a funny look on their faces and act embarrassed, but this boy shot his statement right out as normally and naturally as you please.

Something of this nature happened in my church recently. This church is located in the heart of New York City on Fifth Avenue and the young people came from everywhere in the United States. A young broker from Kansas City came to

New York "to do the town," as he said. He stayed at a hotel near the church. He started uptown, headed for the night clubs, but as he passed the church he saw a sign. Something about it stopped him. It announced a young people's affair that was going on that evening. Back in Kansas City, he was a church man of sorts, and he thought, "I shall just go in here and see what a young people's meeting in a New York City church looks like, and maybe I can give them a few pointers back in Kansas City."

He intended to stay only for a few minutes, but found such a spirit of radiant happiness that it captivated him, and he stayed all evening. He had a mid-western breezy style and ability to get acquainted. As a matter of fact, even an iceberg would have acquired a genial glow of warmth from that crowd. He played around with them all the weekend, and then went back to Kansas City.

When he left he said, "What do you know? I came to New York on business and to do the town, and I got a greater thrill in this church than I ever could have found on Broadway or in the night clubs. I never did get up to the brightlight district. I found all the bright lights I needed right down there in the church."

By changing your thoughts you can also change situations and changing some situations is a requisite to success and happiness. You can develop an almost incredible power that will help you in crises where otherwise you would surely fail. You put too much dependence upon methods other than those of a spiritual nature to give us force and strength. We have not yet learned to believe in the astounding power of spiritual force. The sun quietly and without a sound can accomplish what all the bedlam of the machinery of the world cannot do. Quiet spiritual thinking establishes contact with spiritual energy and thus endows the man who practices it with super-human strength.

On an early morning train running from Cedar Rapids to Chicago, I happened to meet the famous Negro singer, Roland Hayes. He occupied the seat across from me in the parlor car. We had what was for me, at least, one of the most stimulating conversational experiences in my life. The talk turned to religion, the consuming interest of Mr. Hayes. Without question, he is not only one of the truly great singers of our time, but one of our noblest spiritual geniuses as well. He has sung before presidents and kings, and before acclaiming audiences in many lands, but he remains a simple, unaffected disciple of the King of Kings.

He told me that it is his custom as he begins a program to stand quietly for a minute by the piano as the vast audience waits. He closes his eyes and prays saying, "Lord, as I sing, please blot Roland Hayes out. Let the people see only Thee."

"I believe," he explained, "that when I do that sincerely, I become a channel through which God's spirit flows to move and lift the hearers." Critics have long been impressed by the deeply spiritual quality of Mr. Hayes' artistry. Undoubtedly it is accounted for in part at least by his devout attitude. Singing, to him, is primarily a method by which people may be lifted spiritually.

Roland Hayes told me a story that morning on that rushing train that will live with me forever as an illustration of the power of the spirit over any force in this world.

In a certain town late at night, he was set upon by four policemen who manhandled him without the slightest justification. Their attitude was brutal, bordering on the sadistic, and they gave full expression to their hatred not for him alone but for his race. Here was one lone and defenseless Negro at the mercy of four white men unrepresentative of, and a disgrace to, the white race.

"Didn't you get angry and fight them back?" I asked.

"How could I?" he replied. "I was no match physically for even one of them. But I *was* a match for them in another way and so was able to overcome them. I brought to bear a power that no evil can stand against."

"What did you do?" I asked with intense interest.

"I retired into God-consciousness," he replied. "I just prayed for the spirit of Christ to flow through me into the hearts of these misguided men. As I thus exercised spiritual thought-power, suddenly I had a feeling of being lifted up high above this hatred and I looked down upon them in compassion and pity. One policeman raised his pistol with the intent of hitting me with its butt. While his arm was raised a curious and bewildered expression overcame his face. Slowly his poised arm dropped. He had been stopped by the tremendous power of the spirit, by God-consciousness."

Later Mr. Hayes was invited back to that town by the Christian-in-spirit members of that community. He returned as guest of honor at a great tribute meeting. Messages came from the President of the United States and other distinguished citizens.

As the train on which we rode roared through a snowstorm, I sat awe-struck before the spiritual power of this man, for his story was told with a complete absence of self. At times his voice was so low I could scarcely catch his words. I, who try to preach Christianity, sat as a very imperfect student in the presence of a master of the spiritual life.

Roland Hayes had discovered and demonstrated a spiritual method that proved extremely practical. By long practice he had become a master at it and therefore was able to summon the energies of his mind in a crisis. Not being practiced, perhaps we would fumble this skill at first. But if you will discipline and train your mind, seeking constantly to bring it into harmony with the mind of Christ, you, too, in your hours of difficulty will be able to summon a power against which nothing can stand.

Happiness and success therefore depend strangely upon our ability to free our minds to work for us. Anything that inhibits the flow of spiritual energy through the mind tends to defeat us. Men allow their minds to become shackled in many ways—by self-pity, by anxiety, by self-interest, by lust, by greed. Charles Dickens spoke wisely when he said, "We bear the chains we forge in life." We prevent ourselves from attaining our heart's desire by the cruel manner in which we hamper our own minds.

In this book we have tried to outline many of the ways in which the mind can become untangled. Psychiatric science is of great assistance. In our Psycho-Religio Clinic at the Marble Collegiate Church, the distinguished psychiatrist, Dr. Smiley Blanton, and I have worked painstakingly on the problem of eliminating the tangles from people's minds. Sometimes it is a long, slow tedious process. It is often effective, I am thankful to report. There is great effectiveness in the joint operation of Christianity and psychiatry. However, we have learned to rely upon another factor that cures the mind as a surgical operation oftentimes cures organic trouble that has not yielded to long treatment. Perhaps I can best explain this process by applying to it an old and often misunderstood term. This term, however, is the best possible explanation. The term is "conversion," and I take that to mean the inflow into the mind of spiritual power with such potency and therapeutic effectiveness that the mind is completely changed. There is a phrase in the New Testament which is very graphic and which portrays what takes place in this process. "If any man be in Christ, he is a new creature: old things are passed away; behind, all things are become new." (II Corinthians 5:17.)

That is to say, change your thoughts (spiritually) and everything changes. A newspaper editor told of experiencing this process in his struggle with fear. This man, born in Canada of French-Canadian parents, came into the world with a withered leg. From earliest infancy he had to wear a brace on his leg. As he grew, he found that he could not compete with the other boys. If he couldn't run or play or climb trees as a little lad, how could he climb the ladder of life later on, he reasoned.

Thus the poisonous fear began to come into his thought and finally fear created a brace on his mind, even as he had a brace on his leg.

But the father said, "Son, don't worry about that leg of yours. Someday I am going to take you into the cathedral and there before the great altar, God will heal you."

The great day came. Both father and son, dressed in their best clothes, went reverently into the church. They came down the aisle of the cathedral hand in hand, the boy looking about wonderingly, his little withered leg thumping along.

They knelt at the altar. The father said, "Son, pray and ask God to heal you." They both prayed. Finally the boy lifted his face. His father was still in prayer. Then the father lifted his face. The boy said in later years, "I have seen my father's face under many circumstances, but never before had I seen such unearthly beauty as was upon his countenance in that moment. There was a light resting there. It was the reflected exultation of the true believer. There were tears in the father's eyes, but beyond the tears and shining through was the dazzling sunlight of faith. It was a wonderful sight, my father's face," the boy said.

Then the father put his hand on the boy's shoulder and said with deep feeling, "Son, let us give thanks to God. You are healed."

The boy was profoundly impressed. He stood up and then he looked down and there was his leg, the same as before. They started down the aisle, the little withered leg thumping along as usual. The lad was deeply disappointed. They came almost to the great door of the cathedral, then the boy said, "I stopped dead still, for all of a sudden I felt something tremendously warm in my heart. Then I seemed to feel something like a great hand pass across my head and touch me. It was as light as eiderdown but I can feel it to this day, the delicacy and yet the strength of the touch. All of a sudden I was wondrously happy and I cried out, 'Father, you are right, I have been healed. I have been healed.'"

Boy that he was, he was wise enough to know what had happened. He said, "God had not taken the brace off my leg, but He had taken the brace off my mind." God is great enough to heal a withered leg, if it is His will, but perhaps it is a greater thing to heal a wounded mind, a mind which carries the brace of fear. To strike off that brace, so set free the mind so that never again should it be bound and hampered by abnormal fear or any other enemy of success and happiness surely is one of the greatest things in this world. With the mind set free your thoughts change and so—everything changes.